Monk Parakeet

Monk Parakeets as pets.

Monk Parakeet book for pros and cons, housing, keeping, diet and health.

By

Macy Peterson

ALL RIGHTS RESERVED. This book contains material protected under International and Federal Copyright Laws and Treaties.

Any unauthorized reprint or use of this material is strictly prohibited. No part of this book may be reproduced or transmitted in any form or by any means, electronic, mechanical or otherwise, including photocopying or recording, or by any information storage and retrieval system without express written permission from the author.

Copyright © 2018

Published by: PESA Publishing

Table of Contents

Table of Contents 3

Introduction 4

Chapter 1: Understanding a Monk Parakeet 7

Chapter 2: Living with the Monk Parakeet 21

Chapter 3: Breeding Monk Parakeets 40

Chapter 4: Setting the Monk Parakeet's home 46

Chapter 5: Diet requirements of the Monk Parakeet 55

Chapter 6: Health of the Monk Parakeet 67

Chapter 7: Maintaining the Monk Parakeet 83

Chapter 8: Training the Monk Parakeet 91

Conclusion 110

References 111

Introduction

I want to thank you and congratulate you for buying the book 'Monk Parakeet as a pet'. This book will help you to understand everything you need to know about domesticating a Monk Parakeet. You will learn all the aspects related to raising the Monk Parakeet successfully at home. You will be able to understand the pros and cons, behaviour, basic care, keeping, housing, diet and health related to the animal.

The Monk Parrot is also referred to as the Quaker Parrot, Monk Parakeet or Quaker. This particular bird is known to be extremely playful and talkative. It is also very naughty and mischievous. You will be surprised as to how intelligent this bird species can be.

It is well known that a bird as intelligent and playful as the Monk Parrot can be a very happy addition to your family. Your family will love spending time with the bird. But, you should also understand that along with the fun comes great responsibility.

You need to take good care of your bird if you wish the bird to stay healthy and active. It is often seen that the birds that are not cared for slip into various diseases. There are many things that you need to take into account before taking the decision to get the bird.

There are people who are impressed by the adorable looks of the Monk Parakeet. They think that this reason is enough to domesticate the animal. But, domestication of a Monk Parakeet has its unique challenges and issues.

If you are not ready for these challenges, then you are not ready to domesticate the animal. If you have already bought or adopted a Monk Parakeet, even then you need to understand your pet so that you take care of him in a better way. It is important that you understand that owning any pet will have its advantages and disadvantages.

You should see whether with all its pros and cons, the animal fits well into your household. Domesticating and taming a pet is not only fun. There is a lot of hard work that goes into it.

It is important that you are ready to commit before you decide to domesticate the animal. If you are a prospective buyer, then understanding of these points will help you to make a wise decision.

When you bring a pet home, it becomes your responsibility to raise the pet in the best way possible. You have to provide physically, mentally, emotionally and financially for the pet. Before you embark on this journey of raising your pet, it is important to evaluate your resources and make sure that you are ready for the pet.

You should also evaluate the practical side of things. It is important that you know that the cost of bringing up a Monk Parakeet might be more than the cost you would have to encounter while raising a dog or a cat.

It is important to have a thorough understanding about the animal. Spend some time to know everything about the Monk Parakeet. This will help you know your pet better. The more you know about your pet, the better bond you will form with him. Whenever you get a pet home, you have to make sure that you are all ready for the responsibilities ahead.

A pet is like a family member. This is the basic requirement to domesticate an animal. It is more than important that you take care of all the responsibilities for the animal.

If you wish to raise a Monk Parakeet as a pet, there are many things that you need to keep in mind. It can get very daunting for a new owner. Because of the lack of information, you will find yourself getting confused as to what should be done and what should be avoided. You might be confused and scared. But, there is no need to feel so confused. After you learn about the Monk Parakeets, you will know how adorable they are. You should equip yourself with the right knowledge.

It is important that you understand the basic behaviour of the Monk Parakeet. This will help you to understand what lies ahead of you. If you understand how a Monk Parakeet should be cared for, you will make it work for yourself. You should aim at learning about the animal and then doing the right thing for him. This will help you to form a relationship with him.

Once you form a relationship with the Monk Parakeet, it gets better and easier for you as the owner. The pet will grow up to be friendly and adorable. He will also value the bond as much as you do. This will be good for the pet and also for you as the pet owner in the long run.

If you are in two minds whether you need a Monk Parakeet or not, then this book will make it simpler for you. You should objectively look at the various advantages and disadvantages of owning a Monk Parakeet. This will help you to make your decision.

If you are looking to domesticate the Monk Parakeet, then you might be having many questions and doubts. You still might not be sure whether you want to buy the Monk Parakeet or not. If you are still doubtful, then this book is meant to help you make a well-informed decision.

You need to make sure that you are ready in terms of the right preparation. This book will help you in this preparation and be a better owner for your pet.

You will learn many ways to take care of your Monk Parakeet. This book will try to address every question that you might have when looking at raising the Monk Parakeet. You will be able to understand the pet and give it the care that it requires.

You can expect to learn the pet's basic behaviour, eating habits, shelter requirements, breeding, grooming and training techniques among other important things.

In short, this book will help you to be a better owner by learning everything about the animal. This will help you form an everlasting bond with the pet.

Chapter 1: Understanding a Monk Parakeet

The Quaker Parrot or the Monk Parakeet is a small sized Parrot bird. It is bright green in colour and has a grey breast and green yellow abdomen. These birds originate from temperate and subtropical areas of Argentina and also some countries in South America. They are also found in North America and parts of Europe.

This particular bird is known to be extremely playful and talkative. It is also very naughty and mischievous. You will be surprised as to how intelligent this bird species can be.

It is well known that a bird as intelligent and playful as the Monk Parrot can be a very happy addition to your family. Your family will love spending time with the bird. But, you should also understand that along with the fun comes great responsibility.

You need to take good care of your bird if you wish the bird to stay healthy and active. It is often seen that the birds that are not cared for slip into various diseases. There are many things that you need to take into account before taking the decision to get the bird. The bird is noisy. You need to have a good tolerance for noises, missing trinkets and also some degree of messiness.

It is known that Monk Parakeets are very entertaining and lovable animals. They will make a great pet. But, this does not mean that they are deprived of all that they would have found in their natural habitat.

It is very important to understand the requirements of an animal or his natural instincts. The Monk Parakeets also have certain specific requirements that need to be met. You have to understand their specific requirements before you can adopt or buy them.

1. Scientific classification

If you wish to study the classification of this bird scientifically, then the following information will help you:

Kingdom- Animalia

Phylum- Chordata

Class- Aves

Order- Psittaciformes

Family- Psittacidae

Genus- Myiopsitta

Species- M. monachus

Binomial name- Myiopsitta monachus

Binomial name- Myiopsitta monachus

2. Subspecies of Monk Parakeets

The M. monachus, or Monk Parakeets, are a species that further has some subspecies. It is known that the Monk Parakeet has some 2-4 subspecies. They all are grouped under Class Aves and Family Psittacidae.

3. Life span

A Monk Parakeet has a life span of 15-20 years or even 25-30 years. But, there have been instances where Monk Parakeets have lived longer than their average life span. The key is to provide them the right environment and also the right nutrition. This will help them to grow, stay healthy and live longer.

It is also important to note that Monk Parakeets are susceptible to various disease causing viruses and bacteria. Once a Monk Parakeet gets a dangerous and life threatening disease, it can be very difficult to cure him.

The pet Monk Parakeet will require you to pay a lot of attention to its health, be it vaccination or health care. The pet will definitely live longer if you make sure that you do all that is necessary for its health.

4. What does a Monk Parakeet look like?

The Parrot is considered to be a medium sized bird. The Monk Parakeet is some 12 inches in length and weighs between 3.25 ounces to 4.25 ounces. The Quaker Parrot or the Monk Parakeet is a small sized Parrot bird. It is bright green in colour and has a grey breast and green yellow abdomen. Some subspecies of the Monk Parakeet can have colour mutations such as blue, yellow and cinnamon. But, such Quakers are known to be very rare.

The underside of the Parakeet's wings are tinged in blue. The beak of the Monk Parakeet is horn coloured. If you are looking for one distinguishing feature of the Quaker Parakeet, then it has to be its storm grey face, chest and neck. The size and coloration causes them to be confused with the Conures.

5. Ecology and behaviour of Monk Parakeets

The Monk Parakeet has become very popular and also common all around the world. The Parakeet is considered as an agricultural pest in Argentina, Brazil and Uruguay. The bird is known to build a protected nest in an artificial forest. At such places, the ecological pressure and competition from other species is negligible.

This bird is known to make stick nests. The bird can make it in a man made structure or even a tree. The species of these Parrots are gregarious. They breed colonially, where they have big, but a single nest. Each pair has its own entrance. These nests are often very big. They can build nests up to seven feet across. Each pair enjoys a separate space or apartment for itself. These nests attract many bird pairs, often from other species also. The Monk Parakeets also have helpers that help the pair to raise the offspring at various stages.

6. Legal regulations

When you are studying the domestic Monk Parakeets closely, it is important to understand the legal regulations that govern them. This will help you to know how easy it is for you domesticate the Monk Parakeet in your country.

- Brazil: If someone in Brazil wishes to domesticate these birds, then it possible with a few legalities. It is imperative to get the Monk

Parakeets sterilized. And, you will also be required to get the Monk Parakeet a microchip identification chip.

- New Zealand: Since the year 2002, New Zealand has made it illegal to breed and sell these animals. If you wish to domesticate a Monk Parakeet in New Zealand, you will have to go through various legalities to make this possible.

- Japan: Certain places in Japan make it very simple for the owners to domesticate the Monk Parakeets for there are no restrictions. But, some areas will require you to register yourself and the Monk Parakeet with the local body in your area.

- Australia: There are some places in Australia that allow the domestication of the Monk Parakeets. The states may require you to have a legal license to domesticate them. There are some places where the keeping of these animals is illegal. For example, Queensland bans the domestication of Monk Parakeets.

- United States: Previously, the United States banned the keeping and breeding of Monk Parakeets. But, as the Monk Parakeets became popular in the late eighties and early nineties, the laws changed for many places. Many places such as California still don't allow the domestication of Monk Parakeets. Many military bases have banned Monk Parakeets in their areas.

You have to understand the licensing requirements in your area before you can keep a Monk Parakeet. This is important so that you can avert any future issues and problems.

You should make sure that before you make the payment and buy a Monk Parakeet, you understand all the legalities in your area. Your breeder will also help you to understand all the formalities that need to be done.

This is one of the most important steps while looking to domesticate a Monk Parakeet. You should make sure that you inform yourself well about this and speak to all the concerned and relevant people.

Illegal in some states

If you are planning to get a Monk Parakeet, it goes without saying that you need to be sure that your state allows you to keep the same. You should never assume that the state will allow you to keep all kinds of animals.

Different countries have different rules when it comes to domesticating various animals. It is always advisable to know the rules of your specific state well before you get a pet animal. This will save you a lot of unnecessary trouble. You don't want to pay hefty fines after having spent money on the pet animal.

People who are interested in Quakers must know that they are illegal in many states. This can be a shock for many because people would think why would any state ban a harmless bird such as the Quaker. But, this is not true.

In the wild, the Parakeets can be very destructive. They are known to colonise and cause lots of destruction. It is because of this that they are banned in many states. It is illegal to own these birds or sell these birds in such states.

7. Things to know before you buy the Monk Parakeet

As a prospective owner, you might be wondering the costs that you need to prepare for. You might also be thinking as to what is so special about bringing a Monk Parakeet home.

Why should you be so prepared? Why isn't it like getting any other pet? To clear the various doubts in your head, you should understand the nature of the pet and also the costs that you will incur while raising the pet.

Your Monk Parakeet will have various things that will make him unique. There will be specific requirements of the pet. For example, in regards to diet and housing, the animal has some very specific needs. You should be able to understand the needs and then also fulfil them.

As the owner and parent of the pet, you will have to make attempts to fulfil all the needs of the animal. You should also be prepared on the financial front to take care of these needs.

It is better that you plan the costs that you will incur while raising the Monk Parakeet well in advance. This planning will help you to avoid any kind of disappointment that you might face when there are some payments that need to be made. It is better if you plan these costs well in advance, so that you don't get in a fix at the later stage.

Before you are all set to buy the Monk Parakeet and domesticate him, it is also important that you work on all the costs that will go into raising the animal. This section will help you in understanding what you can expect in terms of costs when you are planning to bring a Monk Parakeet to your household.

In the very beginning, you need money to buy the Monk Parakeet. Once you have spent money on buying the animal, you should be ready to spend more money. You can expect to spend money on the shelter, healthcare and food of the animal.

While there are certain costs that will remain fixed, you will also have to be prepared for unexpected costs once in a while. You have to be ready to bear various costs continuously over the years. Being well prepared is the best way to go about things.

There are basically two kinds of costs that you will be looking to incur, which are as follows:

The one-time or initial costs: The initial costs are the costs that you will have to bear in the very beginning of the process of domestication of the animal. This will include the one-time payment that you will give to buy the animal.

There are other costs that would come under this category. The initial costs that you will face when you have decided to domesticate a Monk Parakeet are the purchasing cost of the animal, the permits and the license cost, the vaccines, costs of food containers and the costs of the enclosure.

The regular or monthly costs: Even when you are done with the one-time payments, there are some other costs that you won't be able to avoid. But, these costs can be planned well in advance. You can maintain a journal to keep track of these costs.

The monthly costs are the costs that you will have to spend each month or once in every few months to raise the Monk Parakeet. The costs will include the costs of the food requirements and health requirements of the pet.

The various regular veterinarian visits, the sudden veterinarian visits and replacement of things come under the monthly costs category.

The various costs you can expect

While you are all excited to domesticate the Monk Parakeet, you should also start planning for the costs that you will incur. You can expect to incur the following the costs:

Purchase price for Quaker: You can expect to spend $20/£14.50 to $120/£87.07 to purchase your Quaker. The price will depend on the colour, age and the health of the animal.

You should make sure that you get the Quaker examined medically before buying it home. The examination and tests will also add on to the initial price.

You also have the option to adopt a Quaker. This will help you to avoid the initial purchasing price, though the other costs for raising the animal will remain essentially the same.

If your breeder has taken care of the initial health check-ups, then you should be fine with paying a little extra to this breeder because he has saved you from running here and there to get these important procedures done.

Cage: When you look for a cage for the Quaker, you will realize that there are great options available for cages in pet shops. You can buy a cage for as low as $50/£37.82 and also as high as $500/£378.25. It clearly depends on your choice and your budget. A decent cage can be expected at $200/£147.25.

The cage is a basic requirement for a pet animal. A pet should be provided with a comfortable cage. The cage should be at least four square feet in its size.

It is always better to get a bigger cage for more comfort of the pet. The floor of the cage should be solid. Also, unsealed wood should be avoided. You can expect to spend on an average $200 for the cage of the Monk Parakeet.

Bedding for the pet: The bedding for the Quaker is another important purchase. You can either look to buy fabric or particulate bedding.

If you buy liners, you can expect to spend $30/£22.20 to $60/£44.39 once. If you go for paper bedding, you will have to spend $50/£36.99 to $100/£73.99 per year.

Heat and light source: It is important to maintain the right temperature and light cycle in a Quaker's cage. If this is not done, the pet can attempt hibernation.

You should just make sure that consistent warm temperature is maintained in the cage. The pet can't adjust to varying light cycles. For example, he gets uncomfortable with short days in winter because he is used to the longer days cycle.

Depending on the type and brand of the heat and light sources, you can expect to spend $30/£22.20 to $60/£44.39.

Vet fund: When planning the monthly costs, you can't overlook the cost of visits to the vet. If your Quaker is healthy and fit, even then you should visit the vet at least once a year.

A yearly check-up will help you keep a track on the health and progress of your pet. This yearly visit that would also include some tests, should not cost you more than $60/£44.39. This is a cost that you have to pay once a year, but it is better to plan it well ahead of time.

You should also be prepared for unprecedented visits to the doctor. If your Quaker falls sick, then you will have to take him to the vet. This is something that you won't be able to plan ahead, but you can set aside a certain amount of money each month for the visits to the vet.

It is believed that you should have an extra $1000/£776.2 saved for your Quaker's emergencies. He might require an operation or surgery because of a disease.

It is always a good idea to buy insurance so that illnesses and injuries are covered. You can expect to spend $80/£59.19 per year for the insurance premium.

First aid kit: Though it is always advised to take the pet to the vet if any health problem arises, it is always a great idea to keep a first aid kit ready. This will help in case of minor injuries and also emergencies when you can't reach the vet.

When you keep a first aid kit, it is important that you have knowledge about each item. You should know how to use things. You should also replace stuff when they reach their expiration date.

The various items that the first aid box of the Monk Parakeet should have are bottled water, hand warmers, paper towels, flash light, toilet paper, scissors, tweezers, nail clippers, cotton swabs, hydrogen peroxide, saline water, vitamin A cream, vitamin D cream and Neosporin.

You can expect to spend around $50/£36.99 to $60/£44.39 while preparing a basic first aid box for the Quaker.

Accessories: As an important accessory for the pet's cage, you will have to invest in good quality toys. You also need to buy a hiding place for the Quaker.

Cheap plastic materials that can have an adverse effect on the health of the Quaker must be avoided. Similarly, toys that can be shredded or broken should also be avoided.

Depending on your choice of toys and hiding place, you can expect to spend about $50/£36.99 to $250/£184.97.

Water and food containers: You will have to buy food and water containers for your pet animal. They will be included in the initial costs. It is important that you invest in good quality containers so that you don't have to buy replacement containers in a few months.

The containers should be bought to suit the animal's requirements. You should plan the number of containers that you would need. You could also think about buying an extra water container

There are many people who might feel that this is an unnecessary cost, but you should take out time to understand the importance of good food and water containers.

The estimated cost for the food and water container can be $100/£73.99 to $250/£184.97.

Food: The most important factor that will affect your monthly costs is the food of the Quaker. The type of the food and the quality of the food that you give to your pet will make an impact on your monthly expenditure on the pet.

You will have some options when it comes to feeding your Quaker. You can choose amongst those options, depending on the availability of the items in your region and also the price of the food items.

Each pack that has over two pound of food costs about $10/£7.40 to $30/£22.20.

8. Maintaining hygiene

You should also note that it is not enough to buy a pet and provide him with a cage or food. You also have to understand the hygiene requirements of the pet Monk Parakeet.

Hygiene is always an important factor when you are keeping a pet. The pet's surroundings have to be as clean as possible. This is important so that you can keep your pet away from various diseases.

You will have to make sure that the cage and the surroundings of the pet are clean. You have to make sure that you have the time or manpower to get the cleaning done.

Your pet might defecate on the carpet or floor. While you can litter train the pet, you also have to be prepared for such things. An attempt has been made to cover all the necessary issues that you will encounter when planning to take care of the Monk Parakeet's hygiene.

When you are keeping a Monk Parakeet, hygiene is all the more important. You should make sure that you don't fail to meet the standards that are required to keep the pet healthy.

The habitat of the pet should be as clean as possible because a dirty environment will only lead to germs and diseases. Keep the cage clean at all times, without exception.

You have to make sure that your hands are clean before you can feed the Monk Parakeet. When the Monk Parakeet is sick, you might have to hand feed him. This point becomes all the more important at that time.

Like you would wash your hands after and before eating food, you should maintain a routine of washing your hands nicely with soap before and also after feeding the pet.

These points have been discussed so that you understand the hygiene requirements of your pet Monk Parakeet. This will help you to understand how you can make sure that your pet is living in a clean environment.

When you are looking to maintain hygiene for your pet, you should understand that there are certain tasks that you will have to do once a week or once in fifteen days.

There will also be certain cleanliness related tasks that you will have to do every day, such as keeping the litter boxes clean. You can't postpone these tasks to the next day.

You should make sure that these tasks are done on time and that you dedicate yourself to get these tasks done each time. If you fail to do so, the Monk Parakeet will have to suffer.

9. Bringing home a healthy Monk Parakeet

A major concern that many prospective owners and buyers of the Monk Parakeet is how to make sure that the animal that they are getting home is healthy.

It is extremely critical that you get a healthy Monk Parakeet to your home because once you get an unhealthy bird you will only make things worse for yourself and the pet.

In the excitement of getting a new pet, you shouldn't forget the basic checks that you need to do before bringing the Monk Parakeet home. The last thing that anyone would expect after finding a breeder and getting an animal is that it is not in good health.

You will not know how to care for the sick pet. The pet's health will deteriorate. You will be spending thousands of dollars just on the health of the animal.

The following pointers will help you to make sure that your future pet is in the prime of its health:

- It is very important to bring a healthy pet to your home. You should definitely avoid getting an injured animal home.

- Make sure that you learn as much as possible about the Monk Parakeet before you decide to buy him and bring him to your home.

- Even if the animal has had health issues in the past, it can be a matter of concern for you.

- A younger Monk Parakeet will have issues that could be different from an older Monk Parakeet. You need to make sure that you understand all these issues in detail.

- Check the wings of the bird. If any of the wings are damaged, you should not buy the bird.

- If you are buying an older Monk Parakeet, you need to be all the more vigilant because they could carry some infections.

- First and foremost, you should check the health care card of the animal that you wish to buy.

- All good breeders will maintain a health card, which will have all the details of past diseases and infections. This health card will also help you to understand the vaccine cycle of the animal.

- You will be able to understand which vaccines have been completed and which ones are due.

- It is always better to buy a Monk Parakeet whose vaccines have not been cancelled or missed.

- It is important that you closely examine your prospective pet. You should look for any abrasions on his skin.

- His skin should not be torn or bruised.

- You should make it a point to check the body temperature of the Monk Parakeet. The body temperature should be normal.

- If the Monk Parakeet is too cold or too hot to touch, then there is some problem with its health.

- You should closely look for any kind of injuries. If you find anything that does not seem normal, then you need to discuss it with the breeder.

- The Monk Parakeet should not have any broken limbs. You should be able to check this manually.

- You should look for any hanging limbs. A hanging head or limb could mean that the pet is severely injured.

- Also, carefully inspect the tail and stomach area. There should be no abrasions.

- It is important that the Monk Parakeet is devoid of any infections or diseases when you bring him home.

- It is advisable to take the help of a qualified veterinarian to be sure of the bird's health conditions.

- He will be the best judge of his condition. A good vet will always guide you in the right direction for the Monk Parakeet.

- You should discuss at length about the concerns that you have regarding the Monk Parakeet.

- You should follow all the instructions that the doctor gives you because they will be for the benefit of the animal.

- You should only keep the Monk Parakeet if you are convinced that you will be able to care for the little animal.

- After you have brought the Monk Parakeet home, you should keep him isolated to keep an eye on him.

- You should allow him inside the house only after a few days of checking if everything is normal with the Monk Parakeet.

- In case of any issues, you should consult the vet and the breeder.

Chapter 2: Living with the Monk Parakeet

If you wish to own a Monk Parakeet or even if you already own one, it is important to understand the basic characteristics of the animal. You should know what you can expect from the animal and what you can't.

This will help you to tweak the way you behave with the Monk Parakeet in the household, which in turn will help to build a strong bond between the Monk Parakeet and yourself.

A pet is like a family member. You will be more like a parent than like a master to the pet. You will be amazed to see how much love and affection your Monk Parakeet will give through his ways and actions.

You have to make sure that the animal is taken care of. The animal should be loved in your household. If your family is not welcoming enough for the pet, the animal will lose its sense of being very quickly.

If the Monk Parakeet does not feel wanted and loved in your home, you will see a decline not just in its behaviour but also its health. This is the last thing that you should do to an animal. An animal deserves as much love and protection as a human being.

You should be able to provide the pet a safe and sound home. Your family should be caring towards the pet. You have to be like a parent to the Monk Parakeet. This is the basic requirement when planning to bring an animal home.

All these points are not being discussed to frighten or scare you. In fact, these points are being discussed to make you understand that you have to know the right ways to domesticate a Monk Parakeet.

Monk Parakeets are known to be very loyal animals. If they establish a trust factor with you, they will always remain loyal to you. This is a great quality to have in a domesticated animal.

Along with being loyal, they are also known to possess great intelligence. They will actually surprise you with their intelligence. This makes the pet all the more endearing.

When the Monk Parakeet is in a happy mood, he will jump around the entire space. His unique ways and antics will leave you and the entire family in splits. If you have had a bad day, your pet will surely help you to release all the tension and enjoy life.

They are also very entertaining and playful. You can expect the entire household to be entertained by the unique gimmicks and pranks of the Monk Parakeet. If you are looking for a pet that is affectionate, lovable and fun, then the Monk Parakeet is the ideal choice for you as they won't disappoint you.

If you are still contemplating whether you wish to buy a Monk Parakeet or not, then it is important that you understand all about the maintenance of the pet, so that you can make the right choice for yourself.

1. Advantages and disadvantages of domesticating Monk Parakeets

If you are in two minds whether you need a Monk Parakeet or not, then this section will make it simpler for you. You should objectively look at the various advantages and disadvantages of owning a Monk Parakeet. This will help you to make your decision.

A few advantages and disadvantages of domestication of Monk Parakeets have been discussed in this section. If you are a prospective buyer, then this section will help you to make a wise decision.

There are people who are impressed by the adorable looks of the Monk Parakeet. They think that this reason is enough to domesticate the animal. They believe that just because the pet is tiny, it wouldn't require any maintenance. But, this is not true.

Domestication of a Monk Parakeet has its unique challenges and issues. If you are not ready for these challenges, then you are not ready to domesticate the animal. Once you understand the areas that would require extra work from your side, you will automatically give your very best in those areas.

If you have already bought or adopted a Monk Parakeet, even then this section will help you. The list of pros and cons of Monk Parakeets will help you to prepare yourself for the challenges that lie ahead of you. This list will help you to be a better parent to the pet and to form an ever-lasting bond with your beloved pet.

Advantages of domesticating a Monk Parakeet:

If you are still not sure about adopting or buying a Monk Parakeet, then you should know that there are many pros of domesticating a Monk Parakeet. They are loved by their owners and their families because of some amazing qualities that they possess.

This animal can definitely prove to be a great pet for your household and your family.

The various advantages of domesticating a Monk Parakeet are as follows:

- The size of the Monk Parakeet makes it an ideal choice as a pet. They weigh only a few ounces, which makes them very light in comparison to many other commonly domesticated animals.

- They will actually surprise you with its imitating skills. The bird will pick up some unusual sounds also that are repeated around him. If the bird is kept near the balcony, the bird will pick up sounds of horns of cars.

- The bird has a good observation power and is also a quick learner. This makes it simpler for the pet-owner to train them. They can be taught to talk and imitate human sounds.

- Most people prefer Parrots as pets because of their ability to talk and entertain. These birds are fun to be around. You and your family can have a great time if you have a Monk Parakeet as a pet.

- If you understand how this bird functions in real life, everything will fall into place. You will find it extremely easy to teach the pet and to communicate with it.

- If you are a person who wants his pet to perform various acrobats, then you are in for luck here. The Monk Parakeet is a bird that can be taught some simple tricks. You can teach the tricks to the pet and enjoy the family loving the Parrot performing those tricks.

- You can also show off in front of people who come to your house. The Parrot will make sure that it entertains people with his tricks.

- Their looks make them adorable and cute to look at. They are loved by one and all. Who wouldn't want to have a pet that it beautiful to look at?

- People who love pets that can be lifted and cuddled will love the Monk Parakeet. A Monk Parakeet will allow you to lift it and play with it.

- This bird is known to be a very fast learner. The bird can easily build a good vocabulary by just following the words spoken around him. He will easily catch phrases and use them often.

- The bird is intelligent and can learn to speak very early. The Monk Parakeet is becoming the favourite of families that enjoy a talking bird in the house.

- The bird is highly social. This is a very big advantage for people that are looking for a pet that will entertain them and their guests.

- A Monk Parakeet is capable of entertaining itself. It is very independent in that sense. You don't have to constantly worry about keeping the bird entertained and happy.

- You will be delighted to know that the breeding of the Parrot is considered as one of the easiest in all species of birds. This makes them an ideal choice for breeding enthusiasts.

- Breeders not only find the breeding in this species easy, but also economical. They can easily get Quaker Parrots and then can breed them to get some more. The process is easy and hassle free.

- By nature, the Monk Parakeets are very prolific. They are capable of laying eggs multiple times a year.

- This pet will be the centre of affection for all the family members and also for each and every visitor of the house.

- Monk Parakeets are known to be very loyal kind of animals. They will your presence around them and will show you that they love you by their own unique ways.

- If they establish a trust factor with you, they will always remain loyal to you. Loyalty is a very good trait in an animal. This is a great quality to have in a domesticated animal.

- Monk Parakeets are also known to possess great intelligence. You should be prepared to witness their intelligent antics and gimmicks. They will actually surprise you with their intelligence.

- A Monk Parakeet is a very sharp animal. It is always good to have a pet that is intelligent and sharp.

- If you care well for the pet, he will also respond in a very positive way. When the Monk Parakeet is in a happy mood, he will jump around the entire space. His unique ways and antics will leave you in splits.

- If there are kids in your home, then they will fall in love with this pet. But, you should monitor the interaction of the kids with the pet. This is important to keep everyone safe and sound.

- The Monk Parakeet is a very active and energetic animal when it is awake. Everybody in the house will love the pet. This is because of its very unique nature. The Monk Parakeet will be a very energetic, playful and happy kind of animal.

- The Monk Parakeet can be served store bought Monk Parakeet food. There are easily available food items to ensure that the right nutrition is given to your pet.

- The Monk Parakeets don't overeat, so you don't have to worry in this aspect. You can leave food in the container and the Monk Parakeet will eat as much is required. They are used to eating several small meals.

- Monk Parakeets can be trained against nipping. You can also litter train them. You can teach them some easy tricks to have more fun with them.

- A very important point to note here is that their demeanour will depend a lot on how they are raised. The preparation has to begin right from the start. You can't expect them to suddenly become friendly after years of wrong treatment. If they are raised to be social, they will be very social.

- Monk Parakeets live in groups in their natural environment. This makes them tolerant towards other Monk Parakeets.

- Monk Parakeets have a fairly long life, if they are taken care of. You can make a strong emotional bond with your pet and can enjoy the fruits of the bond for years to come.

Disadvantages of domesticating a Monk Parakeet:

While you have studied the advantages of domesticating a Monk Parakeet, it is also important to learn about the various disadvantages that come along. Everything that has merits will also have some demerits, and you should be prepared for this.

The adorable and friendly animal has his own set of challenges when it comes to domesticating them. It is important to understand these disadvantages so that you can be better prepared for them. Following are the disadvantages of raising a Monk Parakeet:

- The Monk Parakeets are very energetic by nature. This behaviour could be difficult for a first time owner.

- These animals have a very unique temperament, and it would require patience from your side to understand this kind of temperament.

- An important point that you need to understand is that the Parrot needs to be actively engaged. The bird has a lot of energy and if not tapped in the right way, it can be a source of unpleasant mess for everybody around.

- In the wild, the Parakeets can be very destructive. They are known to colonise and cause lots of destruction. It is because of this that they are banned in many states. It is illegal to own these birds or sell these birds in such states.

- You shouldn't be surprised if you see your Monk Parakeet trying out different tricks to get what it wants. They are stubborn. If it wants something, then he better get it. He will try all sorts of means to make sure that he does.

- The pet bird can be very competitive in its nature. This aspect will come out if you have more than one Parakeet. You will notice that the Quaker will get into a fight for everything. The Quaker will fight for food and space. It will compete for toys in the cage.

- These animals are known to eat smaller but very frequent meals. So, you have to make sure that the Monk Parakeet has something to eat every few hours. Such maintenance could be difficult for some people.

- They get sick very easily. A lot of care has to be taken to ensure that they maintain good health.

- They catch disease causing bacteria and viruses very easily. Once infected, it is difficult to treat them.

- The Monk Parakeet has a habit to nip or bite. This is a habit that helps them to interact with other Monk Parakeets, but they can nip you also. Nipping can hurt you, but you can train the Monk Parakeet against such behaviour.

- The food that you serve them might be easily available, but the right brands might not be too cheap.

- They are definitely not suitable for someone who is looking for a quiet and calm pet. They are energetic, will run around and will also make noises.

- Because of his energy levels, the Monk Parakeet can run into things and can get hurt very easily.

- If the Monk Parakeet is lost, it is almost impossible to find it. He will not be able to find his way back to the house. And, the Monk Parakeet is so small that anything can happen to him when it is lost.

- The Monk Parakeet has a tendency to run into danger every now and then. You have to be very serious about Monk Parakeet proofing the house, else you will lose him.

- The animal seeks a lot of attention. The Monk Parakeet is a kind of pet that will require you to pamper him a lot.

- The pet can get stressed and depressed if he is left lonely for longer durations. You can't leave him in the cage for too long.

- You will have to spend a lot of money on the vaccination and healthcare of the Monk Parakeet.

- If spending too much money is an issue with you, then you will have to think twice before purchasing the animal.

- You should also understand the various other costs that you will encounter while raising your pet. You will have to spend a lot of money on their health.

- These animals love playing and running around. These pets are fond of exploring things. They can create a mess if not monitored.

2. Introducing the Monk Parakeet to a new bird

There are many people who want to keep more than one Monk Parakeet at their home, but are scared of the consequences. What if the Monk Parakeets don't get along? What if the older Monk Parakeet gets insecure? If you too are sailing in the same boat and are having the same set of questions, then this particular section will help to clear most of your doubts.

To begin with, you should know that keeping more than one Monk Parakeet in a household is not a bad idea. In most cases, the Monk Parakeets give each other company. A Monk Parakeet can get severely stressed of he is lonely. If there are two or more Monk Parakeets in the home, they give each other company.

Monk Parakeets are used to being with each other in their natural surroundings. They get along well with one another. They'll fight and play and will keep each other entertained.

So, if you are having doubts about bringing home another Monk Parakeet, then you need not be scared. But, you have to be careful while introducing the Monk Parakeets to each other.

If you have made a decision to buy a new Monk Parakeet at a later stage, you will have to take certain precautions. It is always better if you get young birds of about the same age if you are sure about keeping more than one Monk Parakeet. These young birds or chick will grow up together and it will be easier for them to get along.

If you have a Monk Parakeet that is very old and sick, it can be very difficult for him to adjust with a new Monk Parakeet. His health condition and age will make it very difficult for him to adjust to the new life situations.

On the other hand, if your Monk Parakeet is healthy, you can introduce him to a new Monk Parakeet by taking certain precautions.

If you give some time to the Monk Parakeets, they will get along with the passage of time. And, this will also give you some time to understand how the Monk Parakeets are adjusting to each other. There are a basic set of steps to make it easier for the Monk Parakeets.

If you think that you can bring a Monk Parakeet and just leave him with the older Monk Parakeet, then it will get very difficult. The older pet could have territorial issues that you will have to address. Also, the new Monk Parakeet could carry some disease causing bacteria and viruses. You will have to make sure that the new Monk Parakeet does not pass on these to the older one.

The first thing that you need to do when you are planning to bring a new Monk Parakeet home is to get another cage for the Monk Parakeet. You can get a simple cage for him because this will only be his temporary home. You should keep the new Monk Parakeet in this cage for a few weeks.

Keeping the new Monk Parakeet in an isolated cage is important for both the old and the new Monk Parakeet. The new Monk Parakeet will get some time to get adjusted to the new environment around him. If he is a chick, he will need some space and time to understand his surroundings.

The old Monk Parakeet, on the other hand, will be protected from any diseases that the new Monk Parakeet might be carrying. The Monk Parakeet that is bought from the breeder could be a carrier of some disease causing bacteria and viruses.

If the two Monk Parakeets are allowed to interact in the very beginning, this will only mean that bacteria and viruses get transferred and the older Monk Parakeet could get sick.

It is important that the new Monk Parakeet has had all his vaccines on time. Before you bring him home, you should make sure that you check the health card of the Monk Parakeet. This will help you to understand the health condition of the new pet that you want to bring home.

You can definitely prevent your Monk Parakeet from acquiring a disease from the new Monk Parakeet. With the passage of time, if you witness your new pet to be unwell, you should take him to the vet.

After the passage of the first few weeks, you can be sure that the new Monk Parakeet is not carrying any disease. Now, it is time to slowly introduce the pets to each other. But, this has to be done in stages.

If you think that the two of them can be put together and they'll suddenly become the best of buddies, then this is not going to happen.

You should understand that the older Monk Parakeet is already used to a certain life style. He is used to a way of living and also to the people and pets around him. If suddenly, a new pet walks in, it will get difficult for him at various levels. He will try to fight it out with the new Monk Parakeet to establish his supremacy.

This fight for survival and supremacy will not only strain the relationship of the pets, but will also lead to a lot of stress in their individual lives. Monk Parakeets can get stressed by such situations.

As the owner, it is your responsibility to avoid any such situation where your pets have to go through unnecessary pressure and stress.

To make the transition easier for both the Monk Parakeets, you should be slow. After the first few weeks of isolating them, bring their cages closer. You can place the cage of the new Monk Parakeet next to the cage of the older one in way that they can see each other and smell each other.

Once the Monk Parakeets are okay with each other, you can be sure that it'll get better from there. Give them a few days, and during this time don't bring them physically in one area. Just keep them around in separate cages.

Once you see them acknowledging each other, you know it is time to introduce them in a more intimate way. You can now bring them together in an open space. By now, they know of each other's presence in the house.

You need to supervise such meetings. Though they will not harm each other, you shouldn't leave them alone. Do this for a few days.

The introduction period could extend up to many days and weeks. If you see a Monk Parakeet bleeding or being too stressed and scared, then you know that it is time to intervene.

You should also know that the age of the pets will also determine as to how well they get along. It is always easier for younger Monk Parakeets to get along with each other. If the older Monk Parakeet at your home has been there for many years, he will take a lot of time to accept the new Monk Parakeets.

If the new Monk Parakeet is very young, you can wait for a few months before you introduce him to the older Monk Parakeet. This is the best for both of them. You can expect your pets to get jealous when they see you spending more time with the other one.

To balance things out, you should try to spend time with both and should also be very loving and encouraging in your words. They will sense your tone and love. You have to do this so that the Monk Parakeets don't feel lonely and left out.

If the Monk Parakeets seem to enjoy playing together, they will slowly start getting along. A strong indication that the pets are comfortable with each other is when they are curling up together. You might find them all curled up and sleeping next to each other. This is when you can put the Monk Parakeets together in a cage.

But, even this task should be done in smaller steps. Initially, keep them together only for some time. Then, slowly increase. Add news toys to the cage and observe the Monk Parakeets' reactions. Remove the toys that seem to create tension between the two Monk Parakeets.

In most cases, the Monk Parakeets will eventually get along. Monk Parakeets will slowly get to like each other and enjoy each other's company. It is a matter of time before this happens.

But, if your Monk Parakeets are brutal towards each other and refuse to get along even after multiple trials, then you know that they need to be away from each other. There is a slight chance for this, but still you need to be prepared for this.

3. Knowing your Quaker

If you have made the decision to bring the Quaker home, then it is important that you spend some thought on how you will manage to live with the bird.

The Quaker has a relatively large life span. This means that you would be spending a large chunk of your life with the bird. This only makes it very important for you and your family to live peacefully with the Quaker.

You can't expect to dictate your terms and conditions to the bird. There is no way this can work. The only way that can work for you is that you gather enough knowledge about the bird. This will allow you to live in tandem with the new member of the family.

This section and many other sections in the chapters to follow will help you understand your Quaker bird better. This will help you to adjust into the new role that you will take on when you decide to pet a Quaker.

It is important that you understand the specific traits of the Quaker. It needs to be noted here that though most characteristics will resemble the characteristics of a usual and normal Parrot, the Quaker will also have some specific traits that will make it unique.

You need to lay emphasis on these specific characteristics so that you know what you are getting into. The last thing you want is to realise that the Quaker is not for you after getting the Quaker home. This is not right for the bird. It is always advised that a person does enough research to make sure that he knows what he is getting into. This chapter will help you to understand the characteristics of your Quaker. An understanding of the same will help you to make an informed decision.

Fast learners

The Quaker is known to be a very fast learner. The bird can easily build a good vocabulary by just following the words spoken around him. He will easily catch phrases and use them often. You need to keep a check on what the kids in the family teach the bird. The bird would not be able to distinguish right from wrong.

The Quaker is intelligent and can learn to speak very early. In earlier times, Cockatiel was considered as the favourite talking bird. But, now the Monk Parakeet is becoming the favourite of families that enjoy a talking bird in the house.

Manipulative

You shouldn't be surprised if you see that your Monk Parakeet tries out different tricks to get what he wants. The Quaker is stubborn. If it wants something, then he better get it. He will try all sorts of things to make sure that he does.

According to a pet parent's experience, his Quaker has certain smart moves to get what he wants. For example, if he is eating something that the Parakeet is fond of, the bird will kiss on his cheeks and bite on his lips to get a piece of the food. If this does not work then he will sit on his shoulder and constantly repeat the words 'I love you'. This ought to melt the pet parent's heart.

Independent in nature

A Monk Parakeet is capable of entertaining itself. It is very independent in that sense. You don't have to constantly worry about keeping the bird entertained and happy.

Competitive

Your pet bird can be very competitive in its nature. This aspect will come out if you have more than one Parakeet. You will notice that the Quaker will get into a fight for everything. The Quaker will fight for food and space. It will compete for toys in the cage.

You shouldn't be surprised if you see your Quaker bird getting competitive to gain more attention from you and the other family members. The Monk Parakeet will do things that ensure that you have to pay more attention on him.

The Monk Parakeet likes to believe that he is an indispensable part of the family and is very important in the family structure. If he is not made to feel the same way, he will go out of his way to gain attention from the family members. For example, he could make enormous amount of mess with things lying around in the area.

4. Treating the Monk Parrot like a member of the family

You should always treat a pet animal like a family member. This actually goes without saying. But, you need to understand that there are some pet animals that require more attention than others.

Treating the bird like a family member means that you will have to plan family activities around him. The bird should feel like it is a part of the main activity. This will help the Quaker to ease into the new family and new home.

Each animal is different from the other animal. Pet animals are also very different in their requirements and needs. For example, a fish in a aquarium will require different kind of attention than a dog. Similarly, the pet rabbit will have different needs when compared to a pet bird.

It is important the family understands these needs and requirements that are specific to the breed of the animal. An understanding of the same will help the animal to adjust well and will also help you and your family to adjust well to the animal.

5. Engaging the Quaker

Another important point that you need to understand is that the Parrot needs to be actively engaged. The bird has a lot of energy and if not tapped in the right way, it can be a source of unpleasant mess for everybody around.

There are many people who think that keeping the bird's cage at an isolated spot will help the bird to be as ease. But, this is not true. These people fail to realise the basic nature of the bird.

The Quaker bird wants to be at the centre stage. It wants to be able to play a part in all that is going around. In simple words, it wants to be a part of the action scene and doesn't like being a mere far-off spectator.

A few pointers to actively engage the Monk Parrot are as follows:

- You should always keep the cage of the Monk Parrot in the living area where the family spends most of its time. This will give the bird a sense of belonging which is very important to make it feel at ease.

- Always avoid keeping the cage at areas that are not frequented by the family members. You should completely avoid isolated places in the house. The bird needs activity more than it needs peace and quiet.

- It is always better to keep the cage at a specific position. You should try not to change the location of the cage frequently. When you keep the cage at a specific place, the Monk Parrot will slowly attach a sense of belonging to the space. This is ideal and important for the overall well-being of the Monk Parrot.

- Allow the pet bird to spend good amounts of time outside the cage. This is very important for the overall development of the bird. A bird that is forced to stay in the cage all the time will show lapses in its health and mental well-being.

6. Embracing the chaos

We all want our surroundings to be neat and clean. We want to live in an environment with minimum noise. If you are planning to get a Quaker, you need to know that a neat and clean house with minimal sounds could be a distant dream.

You will have to adjust to the fact that these birds are messy and noisy. There is no way you can train them to go against their basic nature. It is you who will have to adjust according to the pet bird.

- If you think that you can't adjust to these things then maybe this bird is not for you. It is important that you think over things many times before getting the Quaker. But, once you have bought the bird it is important that you learn to live well with the Quaker.

- It should also be understood here that the bird will not be messing around or screaming all the time. But, you can expect enormous mess at times. Most Parrots are known to be squeaky and unpredictable. They are known to squawk on many occasions.

The chaos that comes along with the bird needs to be embraced by you and the other family members. It should also be remembered here that along with the chaos, comes a great companion. You will be getting a friend with whom you can spend some great times.

7. Interpreting body language of the Monk Parakeet

It you have a Monk Parakeet or are planning to get one, then you should know that it is very important to have a good relationship with the pet. The Quaker Parrot has a long life span so it would be spending a lot of time with you. This only makes it important that you understand the pet well.

You should make sincere and diligent efforts to learn about the body actions and vocalisations of the Monk Parakeet. The Quaker will try to communicate with you with nasal and vocal sounds. This makes it all the more important to learn more about these sounds.

By learning about the common signs displayed by the pet, you will be able to know whether the bird is sad, happy, scared, angry or tired. When you understand the emotional state of the bird, you are in a better position to help the bird.

When you are able to study the Monk Parakeet in a better way, you will automatically become a better parent. You will able to train the pet better and you will also be able to form a better and everlasting bond with the pet.

- **Gnarling**: This is a way of expressing anger and aggression. The Quaker can show some other visible signs such as dilated pupils and feathers that are raised at the back of the neck. At this time, the best you can do is to leave the pet alone. Your Quaker will want you to do so. Don't try to pacify the bird because it will be fine in some time.

- **Grinding beak**: You will hear the grinding sound often from the Parrot. It can mostly be heard during the night time before the pet goes to sleep.

    The lower mandible of the pet will be scraped or rubbed against the upper mandible to produce a sound of grinding. There is nothing to worry about when you hear this sound. It only means that the bird is feeling safe and secure.

- **Chattering**: When you are training a Monk Parakeet to learn new words, phrases and sentences the bird will be seen chattering. This chattering is a Parakeet practicing those words, phrases and sentences.

    There is another kind of chatter that you might hear from the Monk Parakeet. This is more like a moan. This is an indication that the pet bird is amused. It could be because of some incident that happened around him.

- **Whistling**: You might notice that the bird whistles or sings in a happy tone. It is an indication that the bird is happy. The bird is feeling safe and secure in the environment that has been provided to it, so it is a good sign.

- **Clicking of the tongue**: There are certain signs that the Quaker Parrot will display when it is trying to be friendly with you. You can see the bird clicking its tongue against its beak. This means that the bird wants to be friendly with you. This is like an invitation from the friendly pet and you should take full advantage of this. Make friends with the pet Monk Parakeet.

- **Tucking of the head**: You might notice that the Quaker tucks his head under the feathers. This is a sign that the bird is relaxed, which is a good sign. It might also do something like this when it is agitated about something.

  But, during an agitated condition you will notice that the nape is slightly elevated along with the tucking of the head under the feathers.

- **Biting**: When a Monk Parakeet is teething, it will go through many changes. There will be many emotional changes in the Monk Parakeet. This will cause the Monk Parakeet to bite a lot. You should not get alarmed. Never hurt the pet over this.

  You should know that it is just a temporary change. If a younger Monk Parakeet is biting, it has to do more with the pet experiencing new things such as new textures and new tastes.

- **Wiping of the beak**: You should not ignore when the bird is wiping its beak. It means that the bird is irritated with something and experiencing jealousy. You need to find the root cause of it. This is an expression of displeasure. It means that the pet is irritated. If you think it is you who is irritating him then you need to stop whatever you are doing.

- **Waging of tail**: If you notice that your Monk Parakeet is waging its tail then you should be very happy because it is a sign of happiness and contentment. It means that the bird is feeling warm and happy in your home and in its surroundings. You will notice that the lower end of the tail will move back and forth. It can also be upright.

- **Ruffling of head feathers**: At times, you might see your Quaker Parakeet ruffling his wings. You will also see him fanning the tail. This is an expression of displeasure. It means that the pet is irritated.

  If you think it is you who is irritating him then you need to stop whatever you are doing. At this time, the best you can do is to leave the pet alone. Your Quaker will want you to do so. Don't try to pacify the bird because it will be fine.

- **Stretching**: Parrots are fond of stretching, much like human beings. It is a simple way for them to relax. These birds have to spend most of their time standing on their feet, which can make them tired.

  Now you must be wondering as to how does a bird stretch? A Monk Parakeet stretches by extending one wing and the opposite side foot at the same time. This is called stretching. It is known to be good for the Parakeet.

  The over worked and tired muscles of the Quaker get refreshed by a stretch. The blood circulation of the Parakeet also improves when it stretches and relaxes its body.

Chapter 3: Breeding Monk Parakeets

If you have an interest in the breeding of Quaker Parrots, then this chapter will help you to understand the breeding in Quakers in great detail. This will help you to understand and appreciate your Quaker bird better.

You will be delighted to know that the breeding of the Quaker Parrot is considered as one of the easiest in all species of birds. This makes the Quaker an ideal choice for breeding enthusiasts.

Breeders not only find the breeding in this species easy, but also economical. They can easily get Quaker Parrots and then can breed them to get some more. The process is easy and hassle free.

A Monk Parakeet is sexually mature by the age of 12 to 18 months. The bird is quite young when it is ready for mating. A breeder does not have to wait for too long to mate the Quaker Parrots. A female can lay 5-12 eggs at one time.

This chapter will help you to understand all that you need to know about the mating process of the Quaker Parrot.

Not choosy for a mate

There are many birds that are very choosy when it comes to choosing a partner. This is not the case with a Quaker Parrot. The Quaker Parrot will easily get along with any mate it is provided with. This point is very favourable for the breeder looking for great returns with limited Quaker birds.

Some breeders practice a method that allows the Quaker Parrot to choose its own mate. The breeder buys many young Quakers and keeps together in a big flight cage with ample number of nest boxes.

The Quakers can easily find a suitable match in the large group. It is usually a simple process. It should be noted here that only people with no constraints on money and space can practice something like this.

If you are providing a mate for your Quaker, then you need to get a DNA test done. This DNA test will make sure that you are mating a male and female Monk Parakeet.

Colony breeding

If you are interested in the breeding of Monk Parakeets, you need know that more than one option is available. You need to understand what works the best for you, given your financial constraints and also space constraints.

You can allow the Parakeets to breed in a natural habitat, letting them choose their partners. You can also breed them in a captive setup. This kind of captive breeding is called colonial breeding. You can also keep a single male and female pair in a cage and let them mate with each other.

It has been reported that in a captive setup, male and female in a single cage setup works the best. Colonial breeding leads to a lower number of eggs. It has also been noted that the survival rate of the Parakeets is also very low in this kind of breeding.

Artificial Lighting during the mating cycle

The change of the light cycle helps the Parrot to time the laying of its eggs. Therefore, lighting plays a very important role in breeding of the Monk Parakeets. When you are breeding the Quaker Parrots indoors, you will have to ensure proper lighting to the birds.

To make sure that the birds are productive enough, you will have to use artificial lights indoors to copy the light cycle of outdoors. If proper light is not supplied indoors, the birds can end up being less productive. The survival rate of the younger ones would also drastically reduce.

An important point that needs to be understood here is that if you use artificial lights inside and also let the outside natural light come in, the birds can get really confused. All this will have a bad effect on the productivity rate of the birds. So, to begin with you should make sure that there is no outside light.

You should close windows and use dark curtains. Make sure that there is no outside light in the room being used for breeding. The room should only be subjected to artificial lights inside the breeding area.

You should use artificial lights with timers that are set to ensure sixteen hours of light inside the room. Some breeders manually take care of the artificial lights. But, it is always a better idea to attach a timer to the light. This way the birds remain undisturbed and even you can be at peace.

It should be noted that the amount of light directly effects the productivity of the Monk Parakeets. In their natural habitat, the birds can lay eggs twice a year. But, this is altered when they are bred in captivity.

Sixteen hours of light a day can confuse the bird enough to think that spring time has arrived. This causes the captive birds to be more captive. It is known that the captive birds subjected to artificial lights can lay eggs more than two times a year.

You don't have to worry about the bird overbreeding. By nature, the Monk Parakeets are very prolific. They are capable of laying eggs multiple times a year. The birds lay eggs, raise the babies referred to as the clutches and take a break of over 2-3 month before getting ready to produce the next batch.

It is suggested that you make use of full spectrum light such as the vitalites to provide artificial light to the birds in captivity.

Diet

A breeder needs to be very careful about the diet of a male and female that would be producing. If you are also interested in breeding of your pet Quaker, then you should make sure that there is no compromise on the diet of the birds.

A good diet will give strength to the birds. It will also lead to healthier offspring. The whole purpose of breeding will fail if the birds are not able to produce healthy offspring. Giving a wholesome diet to the producing Monk Parakeets and altering the diet as per the condition of the Parakeet is the key here.

To give the Parakeets the best possible diet, you should make sure that the diet of the birds is sufficiently high in calcium and vitamins. Calcium and vitamins are needed at this age and stage of the Parakeets.

If you want to give a seed diet that is rich in fats, then you would be surprised to know such a diet can lead to deficiency of various vitamins in the body of the birds. It is best to avoid such a seed diet.

It is always advised to take suggestions from people who have kept such birds in your area. You should also talk to reputed breeders in your area that deal with Parrot breeding.

They can help you to come up with a plan that is best suited for your Parakeets, given your locality. There might be certain food items that would not be available in the area that you live.

Experienced people will always guide you better. In any case, you should avoid experimenting on the Monk Parakeets. This adventure can lead to serious issues in your beloved birds. You should also consult a veterinarian in case of any doubt regarding the health of the Monk Parakeets.

If you are looking for a sample diet then we can help with you that. According to a survey conducted, most breeders give a three beans mix to the Parakeets that are producing. This helps them to get the most needed vitamins.

Along with the three beans, you can give the Parakeet carrots, corn and rice. All these food items can be made into a single dish that is easier for the Parrots to eat. This kind of a diet will provide the birds with sufficient amounts of vitamins and also calcium. This can be your go to diet plan in case of any doubts.

You can feed a small amount of this mixture to the Parakeets every day. You can also supplement the diet with the help of good quality pellets and also cuttlebone.

There are many other diet combinations that you can give your producing Parrots. You need to take a call based on what is available in your area and what foods your Parakeets enjoy the most. You can do some safe experiments, such as altering between two or more healthy food types. This will help you to understand what food types your Parakeets enjoy the most.

1. Raising a baby Quaker

It is quite simple to raise a baby Quaker. All you need to do is follow a few thumb rules:

You must never give your baby Quaker medicated food. The best food that you can give a baby is starter feed that that is non-medicated. You have certain brands like Rouge Organic Chick Starter.

Adding electrolyte powder and vitamins in the water that the baby Quaker drinks to help them develop well. Remember that baby Quakers need a lot more water than many other baby birds.

The temperature is very crucial. The chicks are not great with handling heat. It is a good idea to keep it at about 80 degrees for the first three days after hatching. Then, you can reduce it to 65 degrees when they are about 7 days old.

From then on, you can reduce the temperature by about 5 degrees till all their feathers are fully developed.

Make sure that the birds are able to escape the heat. If you see that the wings are drooping and the birds are panting, it means that they are very hot.

The birds should be able to move away if they are too hot. After the birds are out of the brooder, you can give them a heat lamp at night. If the weather is too hot, you can avoid this as well.

Quakers require a lot of shade and should be able to get away from the sun. It is a good idea to add some water to the feed, so that they do not choke. In any case, chicks like to eat food that is wet.

Fresh greens can be used as treats for the birds. It is a good idea to add some chopped greens to the water that they drink. The greens should be fresh. If they are wilted or dirty, then you do not have to worry about any diseases or infections.

The water should be fresh and clean. It is a good idea to have a dish that is deep enough for the Quaker to keep their head submerged. This prevents a condition called sticky eye. The birds are able to clean the nostrils out.

In case of baby chicks, the feathers are not entirely water proof. They will develop oil glands only when they are a few weeks old. The mother usually oils the feathers of the bird to let them into the water. So, if you are artificially breeding them, make sure that you give them time before they are let into the water.

For the first two weeks, you should give them a chick waterier. Then, you can have something a little deeper.

A 2 inch chicken wire should be used for the first two weeks so that the birds cannot get into the water. Make sure that the water is changed often.

When the birds are fully feathered, you can allow them to swim. They should have an easy way to get out of the water, failing which they may drown. Provide ramps that will be easy for them to spot and climb out of.

When the birds are allowed to swim, the enclosure that you keep them in will get messy. Make sure you change the bedding regularly to avoid growth of fungus.

Chapter 4: Setting the Monk Parakeet's home

This chapter is an attempt to help you understand the importance of a shelter or a cage in an animal's life. You will be able to understand the basic concerns while building the cage for the Monk Parakeet.

While it is important to have a cage, it is also important that the cage is of the right size. The advisable dimensions and specifications of the cage have also been listed. This will help you to build or a get a cage that is most suitable for your pet.

Like you need a home, an animal also needs a place and space that he can call his home. A home should make him happy and should be inviting for him. When the home does not provide the comfort and security that it should, it can lead to detrimental results.

There are many owners who might feel that there is no need to set up a cage because the pet can stay indoors. But, you need to remember that even if you are a hands-on parent of the pet, there will be times when the pet would be unsupervised.

There will be times when you will have to concentrate on some other work and the Monk Parakeet would be alone. The cage is very handy at such times because you can do your work and can also be sure that your pet is safe and sound in the cage that you have built for him.

Also, during the night time, it is best for the pet and also for the family members that the pet sleeps in his cage. The pet will get used to the cage and your family members can also sleep without any tensions of your pet being loose in the house.

When you will look for a cage for the Monk Parakeet, you will realize that there are great options available for cages in Monk Parakeet shops. You can buy a cage for as low as seventy five dollars and also as high as one thousand dollars. It clearly depends on your choice and your budget.

1. Building the right cage

When you are building a cage for the Monk Parakeet, you have to make sure that you have provisions for the most basic and important things, such as food and water. The ideal cage will be spacious enough. It will allow the animal to roam around freely and rest well when it wants to.

You can use two big containers for food and water. It is important that the pet has access to food and water at all times. You don't want to be busy somewhere else when your pet is stressed with the lack of water. You can use a water bottle for drinking water.

While you make sure that food and water is available to the pet, you also have to make sure that the containers are not movable. The Monk Parakeet might just kick the containers without realizing that the food and water in them was important for him.

To make things easier for you and the Monk Parakeet, you can attach the food and water containers to the cage. You will easily get the tools to do so. When you attach the containers, the Monk Parakeet can't move them. This will also help you to keep the cage clean and mess free.

The bedding that you choose for the Monk Parakeet should be comfortable. It should not occupy the entire cage because your pet needs some space to roam around also. You can get the right bedding for your pet Monk Parakeet from a pet store that sells Monk Parakeet products.

The best buy for a cage is the one that can be cleaned easily. The cage should be comfortable and fun for the pet, but also easy to clean for you. You can go for a cage that has a bottom made of plastic and also coated wire. Such bottoms can be lifted for cleaning purposes.

But, make sure that the wire can't be chewed by the pet Monk Parakeet. You can also go for the metal bottomed cage, but you need to be extra careful with these kinds of cages. You will have to make sure that such cages are not exposed to faeces and urine, otherwise they will rust. You can buy mats and rugs that can be thrown after use to cover such bottoms.

It is important that the bedding of the pet is soft and comfortable so that he can slide in and feel comfortable. But, make sure that you check the bedding every day to know whether the pet Monk Parakeet has been chewing on its material. This can be dangerous so you need to replace such items.

If you wish to keep two or more Monk Parakeets in the house, then your cage requirements will automatically be changed. You can keep the Monk Parakeets in separate cages. If the Monk Parakeets get along, you can also keep them in a single cage.

You should make sure that the single cage is comfortable for both the animals. There should also be some additional space for the second Monk Parakeet in the cage.

Though the Monk Parakeets are very small in size, they need to be comfortable in their shelter. It should be noted that you need additional space per animal in the cage. If you are planning to keep more than one Monk Parakeet, then you should plan the additional space accordingly.

It is not advisable to keep too many Monk Parakeets in a single cage because it is not that all of them get along with each other. So before you plan the cage, make sure that you know how many animals would be sharing the space. This will help you to keep the right amount of additional space.

2. Cage layout requirements

When you are setting up a cage for the Monk Parakeet, you need to make sure that the cage is set up in a way that is inviting for the Monk Parakeet. The Monk Parakeet should not feel captive or like a prisoner in the cage. If the Monk Parakeet is not comfortable, he will begin to get stressed, which is something that you wouldn't want.

The cage should be built keeping in mind the basic nature of the Monk Parakeet. You can't build a cage that is suitable for a rabbit. You have a Monk Parakeet and your cage should be built keeping in mind his natural behaviour, instincts, likes and dislikes. This is the best for you and also for the Monk Parakeet.

You should understand that just because the Monk Parakeet is a small animal does not mean that you can keep it anywhere. You need a proper cage for him. You should never keep him in a glass environment such as an aquarium. Such places don't allow the flow of air and can cause breathing issues in the Monk Parakeet.

It is important to have the right temperature for the Monk Parakeet. If the temperature is more than eighty degrees Celsius or less than fifty degrees Celsius, it is advised to keep the pet inside the house in controlled temperatures. Nothing is more important than the health and well-being of the pet.

Size

When you are buying a cage, the size that you would go for is a very important consideration. What use is a cage if the bird can't fit in well or if it feels suffocated inside? So, it is important to buy the right size for your beloved pet bird.

A Monk Parakeet will weigh somewhere between one pounds to five pounds. The exact weight will depend on the species. The wingspan is another important consideration while determining the size of the cage that you should go for.

The wingspan of a Quaker can range from 11 to 19 inches. The Parakeet might look very small, but it needs enough space to move around. The bird has a lot of energy that it expends by walking around in the available space. This is actually good for his health for he can avoid obesity.

Keeping the above points in consideration, the cage of the Monk Parakeet should be 20x18x18 inches. If you have a pair of Monks then the size of the cage should be even bigger to give them some space.

Shape

If you are thinking about the right shape for the cage of the Quaker Parakeet, then you should know that there are different kinds of cages available in the retailer's shop. But, not all shapes are ideal for the Monk Parakeet.

You should always go with a rectangular or a square shaped cage for the Monk Parakeet. You should avoid cages that are rounded or circular in shape. A simple thing such as a cage can also add to the life and health of a pet.

A Monk Parakeet is fond of seeking shelter in a corner. The pet might need a corner to feel safe. If the cage is circular in shape, the Parrot will not get a corner. This can confuse the bird, which might affect his health and well-being. The bird could face anxiety and stress because of this.

Temperature

If you wish to know the ideal temperature for a Monk Parakeet, then this section will help you. Your pet Quaker needs to have a temperature of 60-70 degrees Celsius. Some Quakers might also be tolerant to temperatures up to 80 degrees Celsius.

If the temperatures in your area remain around this range, then it is ideal for the pet Quaker. But, if not then you will have to maintain the right temperatures with the help of air conditioners and room heaters.

The cage should be located in an area that has enough sunshine. The cage should also be exposed to good ventilation otherwise it will get very difficult for the Quaker Parrot. Though sunshine is required, the cage should never be kept in an area where it gets direct sunlight. This can be very dangerous for the Quaker Parrot.

3. Decorating the cage with accessories

Besides the basic stuff, such as food and water, it is also important to accessorize the cage well. This is important because the right accessories will help him to feel like he is at home. They will bring him closer to his natural habitat and natural tendencies.

When you are planning the furnishing and accessories of the shelter, then you should make sure that you give the pet an environment that closely resembles his natural habitat. This will keep him happy and spirited. And when the pet is happy, then everything around is good.

When you are looking to place the bedding in the cage, place something that is comfortable for him and smooth on his skin. There are several accessories available these days that will help you to keep your Monk Parakeet happy.

When you bring a pet home, the pet will be scared of the new surroundings. You will have to make all the attempts that will help the pet to adjust in the new environment.

One of the safest ways to welcome a new pet is to provide him with a good shelter. The shelter should be as comfortable as possible. While you might save money of buying a cheap cage, you need to understand what is important for you.

You can keep a mineral block in the cage of the bird. More than an accessory, it is a useful item for the Monk Parakeet. The bird needs something to chew on when it is growing. The mineral block can provide calcium to the pet bird when it chews on it. This is a simple way to keep the pet Parrot engaged and also take care of its health.

You should keep a perch in the cage of the bird. It is a good stress buster and also a relief from boredom. It is suggested that you keep two to three perches for the bird in the cage. These perches should be of different widths. This would work well with the Quaker bird.

The pet is more like a new member of the family, a new baby in the house. So when you buy the animal, you should make sure that you understand the needs of the animal at various stages of his life.

It is better to spend some extra money in the beginning than to see your pet being sad and lonely in the shelter. You should make sure that you understand this before you finalize on a cage for the pet.

A simple way to keep the Monk Parakeet happy is to give him some toys. The Monk Parakeet will love it. This will keep him busy and happy. While the Monk Parakeet enjoys the toys, you can bask in the happiness of your beloved pet.

If you go to a Monk Parakeet toy shop, you will get many ideas for the accessories that you can keep in the cage of the pet. There are many types of bedding available these days that can help your Monk Parakeet to have rest and also fun when he wants. For example, you can get bedding in the shape of a cave. This will be fun for the pet Monk Parakeet.

You also have to make sure that the Monk Parakeet is entertained even at times when you are not around. The Monk Parakeet can get bored easily, which will make him a little aggressive. To keep him occupied, you can keep various kinds of toys in the Monk Parakeet's cage.

The right kind of toys should be bought for the Monk Parakeet. You will get many ideas when you visit a shop that keeps toys for Monk Parakeets. But, it is important that the toys are made of a good quality material. They should not be harmful for the pet. Your Monk Parakeet will take them in his mouth, so they should be of a good quality, else he will develop allergies of the beak.

It is better if the toys are washable. This will enable you to wash the Monk Parakeet's toys every now and then when they are dirty. The harmful bacteria will also be removed from the toys when they are washed.

Also, make sure that the toys can be shredded by the Monk Parakeet. If the pet is able to shred the toy, he will swallow the shreds. This is very harmful and will only invite more trouble for the pet. To avoid all these issues, buy the right kind of toys.

If you are planning to domesticate more than one Monk Parakeet, you can consider buying another cage. This cage could be very simple and basic. The main purpose of this extra cage is to use it when one of the Monk Parakeets is sick. The cage will help you to isolate the sick Monk Parakeet.

A vet will always advise you to isolate a sick pet. This is necessary so that the pet can recuperate nicely in the absence of other pets. He would need some space to himself. What is also important is that he should not transmit the disease to the healthy pets. The isolation helps to avoid such a situation also.

4. Cleaning the cage

Like it is important to clean the house that you dwell in, it is extremely important to clean the cage of the pet. You will not necessarily enjoy this process, but still you have to do it. The pet can't clean the cage on its own, and if it is forced to stay in an unhygienic environment, he will fall sick.

There are certain tasks that you need to do daily, while several others need to be done once a week. If the bedding is soiled, it should be cleaned on a daily basis. Similarly, if the food and water containers look dirty, they should be cleaned and refilled. The litter box needs to be cleared every day.

Once a week, you should clean the entire cage. You should thoroughly clean it with a clean cloth. Remember that the Monk Parakeet should not be in the cage when the cleaning procedure is going on. The litter box needs to be disinfected once a week. The toys of the Monk Parakeet should be washed once every two weeks, if the toys are washable.

The litter box and the floor of the cage can be cleaned with the help of a mixture of bleach and water. The mixture should have 98 percent water and only two percent bleach. This daily and weekly cleaning procedure is important so that the surroundings of the Monk Parakeet remain healthy. The bacteria in the dust and dirt can harm the Monk Parakeet.

While you are busy cleaning the cage of the pet Monk Parakeet, it is important that you check the cage thoroughly. If the Monk Parakeet has littered in an area other than the litter box, then it should be cleared and disinfected properly. You should make it a point to do this check on a daily basis.

You can keep baby wipes handy to clean something immediately. It is important that the cage is free from all bacteria and viruses that are known to cause diseases in pet animals. You should keep some time designated for the cleaning of the cage.

If you are using bleach to clean the litter box, then you should make sure that there are no residues on the box. The Monk Parakeet can try to lick on any residue that he may find on the box or the cage. Bleach can be very harmful and dangerous to the pet animal.

Another point that you need to understand is that you should not use very strong disinfectants. Such products can be very harmful if they ingested even in the smallest of quantities. You should always look for mild anti bacterial soaps and detergents to clean the vessels and the floor.

A simple procedure that you can follow once every week to clean the cage thoroughly is to fill a bucket with clean water. Pour some anti-bacterial detergent that you wish to use. Form a nice lather in the bucket. This can be used to clean the toys and the containers. The remaining can be used to clean the floor nicely.

After you have cleaned the floor with the detergent, use plain water to wash off any sign of the detergent. This will ensure that the Monk Parakeet does not ingest anything harmful.

It is also very important that you let the floor dry completely before you allow the Monk Parakeet to come inside the cage. He could spoil the floor and could create a mess for you to clean again. He could even try to drink any residue that he finds on the floor. To avoid all these hassles, you should allow the floor to dry completely.

Chapter 5: Diet requirements of the Monk Parakeet

As the owner or as the prospective owner of a Monk Parakeet, it should be your foremost concern to provide adequate and proper nutrition to the pet. If the pet animal is deficient in any nutrient, he will develop various deficiencies and acquire many diseases. When the nutrition is right, you can easily ward off many dangerous diseases.

The staple diet of an animal depends on its natural habitat and the food available around the habitat. When you domesticate an animal you can't keep it devoid of its natural and staple food. The digestive tract of the animal is also tuned to digest the staple food. You should always keep these points in mind.

Each animal species is different. Just because certain kinds of foods are good for your pet dog, it does not mean that they will be good for your pet Monk Parakeet also. It is important to learn about all the foods that the Monk Parakeets are naturally inclined towards eating. You should always be looking at maintaining good health of your pet.

Generally, the food given to captive pets is lacking in certain nutrients. It is not able to provide the pet with all the necessary nutrients. If such a case, you will have to give commercial pellets to your Monk Parakeet. These pellets are known to compensate for the various nutritional deficiencies that the animal might have due to malnutrition.

You should always aim at providing wholesome nutrition to your pet. It is important to understand the pet's nutritional requirements and include all the nutrients in his daily meals. To meet his nutritional requirements, you might also have to give him certain supplements.

The supplements will help you to make up for the essential nutrients that are not found in his daily meals. Though these supplements are easily available, you should definitely consult a veterinarian before you give your Monk Parakeet any kind of supplements.

It is very important that you serve only high quality food to your pet. If you are trying to save some money by buying cheaper low quality alternatives, then you are in a bad situation. A low quality food will affect the health of the Monk Parakeet.

You can expect him to acquire deficiencies and diseases when he is not fed good quality food. The cure this is taking the pet to the veterinarian. This in turn will only cost you more money. To avoid this endless loop, it is better to work on the basics. Keep the pet healthy by feeding him with high quality foods, rather than spending money on him by taking him to the veterinarian.

1. Providing the Quaker with a varied diet

The food that you give to your Monk Parakeet should be capable of meeting its entire nutritional requirement. The food should appeal to the pet in terms of taste. He should want to eat it, and at the same time it should also provide the pet with all the necessary nutrients.

Meeting the nutritional requirements of the pet can be the biggest concern while looking to domesticate a pet Monk Parakeet. You have to make sure that you understand the diet requirements of the Monk Parakeet before you can decide to domesticate it.

If you have a Quaker Parrot or are planning to get one, then you should remember that you need to give a good diet to the pet so that the pet shows good growth. A good diet is required for both its physical well-being and also mental well-being.

In the wild, the Monk Parakeet will feed on fresh fruits and vegetables that are available to him. The Parakeet will also feed on various seeds such as sunflower seeds if these are available. It is important that a similar diet is given to the pet bird in captivity.

As a pet parent to a Quaker, you are in luck because the pet loves to eat different kinds of food, so you will clearly have many options when planning the diet chart for the bird. The key is that the food that you give the pet should be nutrient rich and easy to digest. The pet should also enjoy what it eats.

The ideal diet of the Quaker will have a mix of fresh foods, vegetables, seeds and pellets. This kind of a mix will keep the bird happy and healthy. What more can a pet parent really ask for?

Quaker pellets

There are commercial Quaker pellets available online and in various markets and retailers these days. These pellets help to give wholesome nutrition to the pet. If you invest in good quality pellets, you can expect to enjoy good health of the pet Quaker for many years. This is how good the Quaker commercial pellets are.

It should be noted that the Monk Parakeets that are kept as pets need to be given these pellets as seventy percent of the diet share. These pellets are made to meet all the necessary nutritional requirements of the Quaker.

A Quaker bird can have about two to three tablespoons of pellets per day. This will make up to 30 to 40 ml of pellets. You should always check the printed guidelines on the back of the pellet box. It is important that all the manufacturing guidelines are met.

While the Quaker pellets are important, it is also important that you do not overdose the poor pet with the pellets. An overdose will do more harm than good. It is also recommended that you consult a veterinarian in case of any doubt.

Never do something that you are unsure of. If you have your doubts about the pellets or the diet of the Quaker in general, it is suggested that you talk to the vet.

Fresh fruits

Parrots are known to enjoy fresh fruits. You will see your pet Parrot enjoy fruits til its heart's content. This makes it important to include them in the diet of the bird. This section will help you to understand which fruits are good for the Monk Parakeet.

The fruits that can be given to the pet Monk Parakeet are apples, pineapples, melons, pears, oranges, berries, kiwi, grapes and bananas. You should remove the seeds of the apples before serving them to the pet.

Vegetables

Parrots are known to enjoy vegetables. Vegetables provide some essential minerals and vitamins to the Quaker that are good for its overall development.

This makes it important to include them in the diet of the bird. This section will help you to understand which vegetables are good for the Monk Parakeet. The key here is that the pet should be able to chew on the vegetable easily. You don't want to give the pet anything that it cannot eat happily.

The vegetables that can be given to the pet Monk Parakeet are corn, kale, lettuce, leafy greens, tomatoes, peas, broccoli, carrots, cauliflower, beans, asparagus, spinach and parsley.

Seeds

It is known that the Quaker parts will feed on seeds available to him. It has been noticed these seeds are not always available to them. So, the Parrots are used to not eating too many seeds. This should be kept in mind when you are planning the diet chart of the pet Parakeet bird.

Seeds when included in the diet of the bird can help him retrieve some important nutrients. But, a diet rich only in seeds will not do the Parrot any good.

A diet that is high only in seeds will not give the Parakeet enough nutrients that are needed for his healthy well-being.

You should focus on supplementing the diet with high quality seeds rather than making these seeds the main component of their diet. Some people commit this mistake of giving too many seeds to the bird. The bird's health will decline if the pet does not get enough nutrients for a healthy survival.

You should aim at giving a tablespoon of 15ml of seeds as a daily supplement to the Monk Parakeet. This will help the bird to attain good health.

It is known that these seeds are very high in energy. They are high calorie foods. They also have good amounts of fat in them. A bird in the wild that flies around will be able to utilise the calories in the seeds.

On the other hand, a captive bird does not need too much fat or energy. This is because he won't be flying a lot. This means that the calories will not be utilised. This should be kept mind. This is exactly the reason why it is advised to limit the seeds in the diet of the pet Parakeet. You can give seeds such as sunflower seeds.

Not all seeds are good for the Monk Parakeet. You should never feed apple seeds to the Parrot. It has been observed that the apple seeds are toxic to the pet bird. He will show signs of food poisoning if such things are given to him.

2. Feeding schedule

As explained earlier, the Quaker pellets need to be given every single day to the pet Quaker. To give the pet optimal nutrition, you should also give it fresh fruits and vegetables. You can keep a small dish in which you can serve the food to the Quaker Parrot.

It is important that the pellets are of high quality and that the fruits and vegetables are unspoiled and as fresh as possible. Don't think just because the pet is a bird, it can eat spoiled food also. Spoiled food will only harm its health.

The Monk Parakeet needs food throughout the day. It is important to set a feeding schedule so that the bird doesn't eat less or more than required. Once the schedule is set, the bird will also adjust accordingly.

You should give fresh food in the Parrot's dish to the pet every single morning. You can keep the dish in the cage. You should also give little amounts throughout the day. It is important that the food that the pet does not eat is removed from its cage. Don't keep the food in the cage to rot. This can be a cause of many diseases.

You should be able to rotate food for the Parrot. This means that the bird should be able to enjoy different vegetables or fruits every second day. The

Parrot can get bored with the same kind of food, so it is important that the food is rotated regularly.

Because your pet is a social animal, it will feel left out when you and your family sit to have your meals. To make the Quaker Parrot feel a part of the family, serve him a small portion of vegetables or fruit when you are enjoying your meals. The Parrot will love this kind of treatment.

You should also make sure that the bird has access to drinking water at all times. The water should be clean and fit for the bird. You can keep the water in a small basin and can keep the basin in the cage of the pet.

But, the bird might soil the water by taking a bath in it or can spill the water by just knocking the basin.

To avoid any such incidents, you can use a water bottle to keep the water of the pet. A bottle for the Monk Parakeet will be available easily online or otherwise. It is a good investment because the bird won't be able to soil the water or spill the water. It will only use the water bottle when it is thirsty and really wants to drink some water.

3. Diet for Quakers ready for breeding

A breeder needs to be very careful about the diet of a male and female that would be producing. If you are also interested in breeding of your pet Quaker, then you should make sure that there is no compromise on the diet of the birds.

A good diet will give strength to the birds. It will also lead to healthier offspring. The whole purpose of breeding will fail if the birds are not able to produce healthy offspring. Giving a wholesome diet to the producing Monk Parakeets and altering the diet as per the condition of the Parakeet is the key here.

To give the Parakeets the best possible diet, you should make sure that the diet of the Parrot birds is sufficiently high in calcium and vitamins. Calcium and vitamins are needed at this age and stage of the Parakeets.

If you want to give a seed diet that is rich in fats, then you would be surprised to know such a diet can lead to deficiencies of various vitamins in the body of the birds. It is best to avoid such a seed diet.

It is always advised to take suggestions from people who have kept such birds in your area. You should also talk to reputed breeders in your area that deal with Parrot breeding. They can help you to come up with a plan that is best suited for your Parakeets, given your locality. There might be certain food items that would not be available in the area that you live.

Experienced people will always guide you better. In any case, you should avoid experimenting on the Monk Parakeets. This adventure can lead to serious issues in your beloved birds. You should also consult a veterinarian in case of any doubt regarding the health of the Monk Parakeets.

If you are looking for a sample diet then we can help with you that. According to a survey conducted, most breeders give a three beans mix to the Parakeets that are producing. This helps them to get the most needed vitamins.

Along with the three beans, you can give the Parakeets carrots, corn and rice. All these food items can be made into a single dish that is easier for the Parrots to eat.

This kind of a diet will provide the birds with sufficient amounts of vitamins and also calcium. This can be your go to diet plan in case of any doubts.

You can feed a small amount of this mixture to the Parakeets every day. You can also supplement the diet with the help of good quality pellets and also cuttlebone.

There are many other diet combinations that you can give your producing Parrots. You need to take a call on based on what is available in your area and what foods your Parakeets enjoy the most. You can do some safe experiments, such as altering between two or more healthy food types. This will help you to understand what food types your Parakeets enjoy the most.

4. Foods that need to be avoided

There are certain kinds of food that are known to be toxic to the Monk Parakeet. The bird will gain nothing when given such foods. In fact, it will show symptoms of poisoning or toxicity. You should make sure that you avoid such foods at any cost.

The following foods need to be kept away from the Monk Parakeet:

- Avocados

- Chocolate

- Apple seeds

- Comfrey

- Onion

- Garlic

- Candies

- Peanuts

- Stone fruit pits

5. Introducing new foods and switching foods

When you get a Parakeet home, one of the biggest concerns that you will have is regarding its diet. It would take you time to understand the diet preferences of the new Monk Parakeet. Monk Parakeets form their preferences quite early in their lives. It is said that in the first six months, the Monk Parakeet has his food preferences.

This means that the first six months is a great time for you to introduce different kinds of foods to the Monk Parakeet. This will help him to have his preferences and will also make things easier for you. If your Monk Parakeet likes three kinds of food items instead of one, it gets easier for you also.

In case a certain food item is not available, you know that you have other choices. If you don't introduce new foods to the Monk Parakeet, he will turn out to be a very fussy. And, you the parent will have a hard time keeping his taste buds happy.

If you want to introduce new foods or switch foods, you can't suddenly change his usual meal plan. This will put off the Monk Parakeet. There are some simple tips and tricks that you should be following to make sure that the pet is eating well even when new foods are being introduced.

A simple way of introducing new food in the diet of the Monk Parakeet is by starting out with a small amount of the food. Take a bowl and add the usual food of the pet in it. Now, take a very small amount of the new food that you wish to feed your pet in the bowl. Mix the contents and serve the food to the Monk Parakeet.

You should know that your Monk Parakeet can outsmart you easily in this case. He will eat the usual food and might just leave the new food. This is because the new food item is alien to him. He needs time to get used to it. But, there is nothing to worry about even if the pet leaves the new food in the beginning.

Just keep adding a very small amount of the food item in the usual food of the pet. Initially, the Monk Parakeet will get used to the smell of the new food. This might take some time so be prepared for it. Once you see that the pet Monk Parakeet has started eating the new food along with the usual old food, you can gradually increase the portion of the new food and decrease the portion of the old usual food.

Another trick to get the Monk Parakeet accustomed to the smell of the new food item is by keeping the old and new food together. For example, you can store the two foods together in a container or in a zip lock.

When you do this, the smells will get intermingled. So, now even when you serve the pet with the usual food, you are serving him the smell of the new one.

The given process will take some days, but you will have to have some patience. The idea is to help the Monk Parakeet get used to the scent of a food before you can expect the pet to eat the food. Once he is okay with the scent, he will try out the food item on his own.

If you are looking for another trick to introduce new food item and switch between food items, then there is another one for you. Take some water in a bowl and add the two food items in the bowl. You can keep the quantity of the old food item a little more than the new one. Now, just stir this mixture and heat it for some time.

Don't heat the mixture of the food items for too long. You just need to heat it for seconds so that the smells blend with one another. When you serve this food mix to the Monk Parakeet, it is like a treat for him.

He will waste no time in eating and licking the food. In the process, he will also eat the contents of the bowl. This is a simple trick to make your pet eat new foods. This trick is also useful when the Monk Parakeet is sick and is refusing to eat anything.

A point that should be noted here is that you should throw away the contents of the bowl that your pet does not eat. Don't keep it to serve him in the next meal. This is because the water will cause the food items to spoil if they are kept for too long.

6. Treats

Treats are an essential part of a pet's meal plan. Treats are like small meal gifts that make the pet happy and delighted. The anticipation of getting a treat can also keep his behaviour in check.

You should work on giving your pet high quality treats. The treat should be tasty and also nutritious. The Monk Parakeet should look forward to receiving a treat from you. This section will give you an idea of the kind of treats you can include in your Monk Parakeet's meal plan.

It should be noted that just because your Monk Parakeet seems to enjoy a treat, you can't give the food item to him all day long. You will have to keep a check on the amount of treats a Monk Parakeet will get. This is important because treats are not food replacements. They are only small rewards.

It is also important that the pet Monk Parakeet associates the treat with reward. He should know that he is being served the treat reward for a reason. You should also make sure that the treats are healthy for the pet.

If you keep serving him the wrong kinds of treats, it will only affect his health in the long run. This is the last thing that you would want as a parent of the pet.

This section will help you understand various kinds of treats that you can serve your pet.

You should always look for treats that are healthy for the pet. The pet should enjoy eating them, but their nutrition should not be compromised. What is the fun of a treat if it is followed by multiple veterinarian visits? Your main aim should be to satisfy the pet's taste buds and also provide him some nutrition.

You should also make an attempt to understand what is there in the treat that you prefer for the Monk Parakeet. If you know the contents and their exact quantities, it will only get easier for you to make a well informed decision. Various pet shops will have Monk Parakeet foods that will help you to make a decision regarding the pet's treats.

The treat should have the right mix of vitamins, fatty acids, minerals and proteins. This will make the treat healthy and wholesome. It is better if the treat has no sugar contents. This is because the sugar will add no food value to the treat. Such healthy treats can be given to the pet Monk Parakeet on a daily basis without any issues.

As a rule, stay away from sodas, dairy products that are not for lactose intolerance, candy bars, chocolate pieces, caffeine, nuts and excessively salty and sugary foods.

These food items can cause some serious damage to the Monk Parakeet. For example, if a nut gets stuck in the digestive tract, it can even kill the Monk Parakeet. Excessive amounts of sugar can directly affect the work of the pancreas and the blood sugar level in the body.

Dairy products are known to cause gastro-intestinal issues in these animals. Also, a large amount of salt is unhealthy for the Monk Parakeet. He can get really sick if you feed him with foods such as chips.

The following treats will definitely be enjoyed by your pet bird:

- Cooked oats

- Cooked brown rice

- Whole wheat bread

- Cornbread

- Yogurt
- Egg noodles
- Cooked chicken
- Cooked turkey
- Cottage cheese

Chapter 6: Health of the Monk Parakeet

To make sure that the Parrot remains in the best of its health; you have to make sure that you understand all the health issues a Parrot can suffer from. You should know ways to detect these issues and also ways to prevent them. This will help you to keep your pet as healthy as possible.

It is known that most of the diseases that your pet bird can suffer from are air borne. This simply means that these diseases can pass through the air.

This chapter will help you to understand all the health issue your pet bird can suffer from. You will also understand simple ways to prevent these diseases. You should also know that air borne diseases are difficult to prevent.

It is advised that you see a doctor when you see your pet having any issue. Any time you see the pet not behaving as normal, you should take professional help. This is the best way to rule out any potential danger.

An unhealthy pet can be a nightmare for any owner. The last thing that you would want is to see your pet lying down in pain. Many disease causing parasites dwell in unhygienic places and food. If you take care of the hygiene and food of the Monk Parakeet, there are many diseases that you can avert.

You should make sure that you do your best to prevent diseases by taking all the necessary precautions. If proper care is given to the food served to the pet, many diseases can be avoided.

You should always make sure that your pet Monk Parakeet is always kept in a clean environment. A neat and clean environment will help you to keep off many common ailments and diseases.

Apart from this, you should take him for regular check-ups to the veterinarian. This is important so that even the smallest health issue can be tracked at an early stage.

At times, even after all the precautions that you take, the pet can get sick. It is always better to be well equipped so that you can help your pet. You should always consult a vet when you find any unusual traits and symptoms in the pet.

You should understand the various health related issues that your pet Monk Parakeet can suffer from. This knowledge will help you to get the right treatment at the right time. It is also important that you understand how you can take care of a sick pet. This knowledge will help you to keep your calm and help the sick Monk Parakeet.

1. Various symptoms of a sick bird

The health of your Quaker is your responsibility. If you are unable to take good care of your birds, they may become infected or may even die. The most difficult thing with diseases related to Parrots is that they spread to the entire flock even before you can notice it. So, you must be vigilant and watch out for some obvious signs that will tell you that your bird is unwell.

The good thing about Parrots is that they have very unique characteristics and behaviour patterns. Any deviation from normalcy is a sign that your bird is either unwell, or is stressed for various reasons. There are some common symptoms that you must look out for if you suspect that your bird has fallen sick:

- Reduced levels of activity
- Not socializing. A sick bird will keep to itself and will occupy a lonely corner in the pen
- Loss of appetite
- Sudden deviation from normal activity
- Sticky poop
- Eyes that are dull or half closed
- Change in the colour of the poop or diarrhoea
- Sleeping for long hours
- Constant sneezing
- Puffed up feathers
- Feathers that are ragged and not preened properly.

- Sudden weight loss

- Swelling in the joints

- Breathing with the mouth open

2. Common health issues

The avian medical history shows that the viruses that infect the Parrots can be very fatal. There is no way you can be lax about your Quaker's health. You have to be on the lookout for any symptoms.

This section will help you to understand the various viruses and infections that can infect to your pet Quaker. You will also learn about ways to keep your pet healthy.

Monk Parakeets are prone to certain diseases such as beak and feather diseases. If proper care is not taken, you will find your pet getting sick very often.

This section will help you to understand the various diseases that a Monk Parakeet can suffer from. The various symptoms and causes are also discussed in detail. This will help you to recognize a symptom, which could have otherwise gone unnoticed.

Though the section helps you to understand the various common health problems of the Monk Parakeet, it should be understood that a vet should be consulted in case of any health related issue. A vet will physically examine the pet and suggest what is best for your pet Monk Parakeet.

The various diseases that your Monk Parakeet can suffer from are as follows:

Beak and feather syndrome

Your Quaker Parrot is at the risk of a beak and feather syndrome commonly known as PBFDS. The Quaker infected by this disease shows some abnormal growth of its feathers. This is one symptom that should not go unnoticed.

The disease can be spread by dried faeces and also by feather dust. You can notice gnarled and swollen shafts in the Quaker. The beak of the Parrot

Quaker will also be severely infected. You can lookout for various symptoms on the beak also.

It is generally noticed that Monk Parakeets at the age of 3-4 years suffer from this disease. But, in many cases Monk Parakeets below the age of three have also known to suffer from the disease.

Remedy

In some cases, the bird is kept on a strict dose of certain medication. But, it should be noted here that this is not the permanent cure for the infection. This will definitely help to control the symptoms, but this is not a permanent cure.

If you wish to cure the pet fully then the effected part will have to be removed from the animal's body. After that medication would have to be provided to help the other part of the gland to recover and function properly.

The disease and its treatment can have complications depending on the kind of infection and also on the location of the virus.

Pacheco's virus

This avian disease is believed to be very dangerous. It is known that this virus is responsible for the death of many birds every year. It is important that you learn all about this virus and its effects.

Pacheco's virus can cause a disease in Parrots that is known as PPD (Pacheco Parrot Disease).

This virus is known to be a herpes virus and is known to occur in South America. The incubation period by this virus is known to be 4 to 14 days. It severely damages the liver. The damage is too fast and usually there are no visible symptoms. This makes the disease all the more deadly.

To be able to catch the occurrence of this disease, you need to keep a vigilant eye on your pet Quaker Parrot. In some of the cases of PPD, the Parrot can suffer from acute diarrhoea. The Parrot will be seen vomiting all that he eats. You can also see the faeces change colour from a bright yellow to a bright green.

It is important that such changes that you witness are not taken lightly. You need to be serious if you need to keep the pet healthy.

As the disease advances, you will notice some neurological disorders in the pet Quaker Parrot. It should also be noted that there are some Quakers that might not get directly affected by the disease. But, these Quaker Parrots can still be the carriers of the virus.

It is always suggested that proper quarantine methods are adopted by pet owners when they get new birds. Diseased birds should be kept away and not in contact with the healthy birds.

Remedy

This section will help you to understand the various ways to prevent and cure the disease. As discussed above the disease is so sudden that there are no definite ways to cure the disease. This is also because there are no symptoms visible to the eye.

One treatment that is popular is to administer the drug Acyclovir to the infected Quaker every eight hours. This can help the pet to get better over time. This treatment is said to be expensive. The bird can also take some time to take to this drug.

Insulinomas

Low blood sugar condition in Monk Parakeets leads to a condition called Insulinomas. When the Monk Parakeet develops a condition in which he has an abnormal growth over his pancreas that releases insulin, it is referred to as Insulinomas.

The release of this insulin in the blood stream leads to a condition of low blood pressure or hypoglycaemia in the animal. The beak of the Parrot will show abnormal growth.

It is also important to note that these growths could either be malignant or non-malignant in nature. If the condition is not treated, it can get very serious and can even lead to the animal's death. A Monk Parakeet at the age of more than three is susceptible to this disease.

- You should be on the lookout for the energy levels of the Monk Parakeet. If he sleeps more than his usual sleeping hours and is lethargic, you should know that something is wrong. Talk to his veterinarian and get his blood test done.

- The exact cause of this health condition is still not known. But, in most cases it has been noticed that this disease either accompanies or follows the adrenal disease.

- Because this disease is related to the pancreas, this condition is definitely affected by the kind of simple carbohydrates the pet is fed.

- The high amount of sugar in the diet of the Monk Parakeet could also be a precursor to the disease. It is often advised that a Monk Parakeet should be served with a protein rich diet.

- You should limit the carbohydrates and sugar and increase the amount of proteins in the pet's diet. Even the treats that are served to the pet Monk Parakeet should be healthy and not just sugar candies.

If you don't provide adequate amounts of protein in the diet of the animal, you will see him suffering from many ailments. There is no proof that a high protein rich diet can help you to avoid this condition, but it will definitely help in the Monk Parakeet's growth and development.

You can look out for the following symptoms in the Monk Parakeet to know that he is suffering from this particular disease:

- You will notice the Monk Parakeet to be very lazy and lethargic. It will appear that he has no energy to do anything.

- He will sleep a lot. If you try to wake him up, he can be unresponsive.

- Your pet will experience disorientation. He will not feel or seem coordinated in his actions or movements.

- The Monk Parakeet will drool around the mouth and might also vomit occasionally. The pet will lose his appetite and will not show any interest in eating his food. He might also detest his favourite foods.

- Another symptom that can help you understand that your pet is suffering from Insulinomas is that he will experience seizures. You will notice sudden and jerky movements in the limbs of the pet. This could be accompanied by sudden passage of urine. He can also make sounds while he is sleeping.

Remedy

One of the first things that you need to do when you see the pet suffering from a seizure is to apply Karo syrup all over his gums and beak. This syrup will help the pet to come out of a seizure that is related to hypoglycaemia.

But, application of the Karo syrup is by no means a permanent fix to the Monk Parakeet's problem. This is only a temporary relief to the poor pet.

Even after the temporary relief, you can expect another seizure very soon. This is because of the increased production of insulin in the Monk Parakeet. You should visit the veterinarian as soon as possible to get the Monk Parakeet tested. The vet will also give medication of Prednisolone to make sure that the blood sugar is stabilized.

He might also suggest surgery to operate on the growth on the pancreas. But, a major problem is that Insulinomas can reoccur. There is no permanent cure for this health condition.

Another complication that can arise from Insulinomas is that it can spread from the pancreas to other organs. This can be very detrimental to the Monk Parakeet's health.

In most cases, the vet advises a surgery and continued medication for the pet. You would also have to ensure that you feed the pet with high protein and low carbohydrates in his meals. He should be fed frequent meals.

Blocked gizzard

Blocked gizzard is a very common problem in Monk Parakeets. It is even said that it is one of the main causes behind premature death in Monk

Parakeets. This condition occurs when the Monk Parakeet has a case of swollen intestinal tissue.

A Monk Parakeet might accidentally swallow something dangerous for him, such as a foam or rubber piece. This will cause the blockage of the digestive tract in the Monk Parakeet.

The best way to avoid such incidents is to always keep an eye on the pet. The Monk Parakeet is a curious bird. He would always be running into some kind of trouble if you don't have an eye on him.

You should make sure that all dangerous items, such as rubber items and foam items are not in the reach of the pet. Keeping dangerous things out of the sight of the pet is probably the best way to avert all the tension that arises following a gastrointestinal blockage. Such a blockage ruptures the intestine tissue, making digestion of food very difficult for the pet.

You can look out for the following symptoms in the Monk Parakeet to know that he is suffering from this particular disease:

- The pet will lose his appetite. You will find him avoiding even his favourite foods. He will not drink water, which could further lead to dehydration.

- You will notice a sudden and drastic weight loss in the pet.

- Another symptom of this disorder is vomiting. The pet will throw up from time to time.

- The pet would be seen struggling during his bowel movements. You should watch out for this symptom.

- You will notice the Monk Parakeet to be very lazy and lethargic.

- The pet will suffer from diarrhoea.

Remedy

If you find any of the above symptoms in a Monk Parakeet, it is important that you waste no time and take the pet to the veterinarian. The vet will conduct X-rays and ultrasounds to confirm the blockage. Don't make the mistake of treating the pet at home.

Usually the symptoms start with vomiting. Severe dehydration follows the bouts of vomiting. If there is a blockage, the Monk Parakeet would need surgery. It is important that you are mentally prepared for this.

Lymphoma or Lymphosarcoma

Your Monk Parakeet is also at risk of another disease called Lymphosarcoma. This disease is also called Lymphoma. It occurs because of the uncontrolled growth of the cells in the Monk Parakeet's body.

Though this is very common in these animals, it can be difficult to detect, especially in the earlier stages.

Monk Parakeets of age four and above are at the risk of Lymphoma. But, it is also known that a type of Lymphoma can also attack younger Monk Parakeets. You should never take any symptom lightly and should visit the vet when you observe changes in a Monk Parakeet.

The vet will conduct tests on the blood sample of the pet to confirm this health condition.

You can look out for the following symptoms in the Monk Parakeet to know that he is suffering from this particular disease:

- You will notice a sudden and drastic weight loss in the pet.

- You will notice the Monk Parakeet to be very lazy and lethargic. It will appear that he has no energy to do anything.

- The pet will suffer from diarrhoea. The lymph nodes of the pet will also be swollen.

- Another symptom that could accompany this disease is a cough. The pet will experience some difficulty in his breathing and will acquire a bad cough.

-

Remedy

The treatment that is available for Lymphoma is chemotherapy. This in no way means that the pet will be disease free. The disease can reoccur in about seven months.

It is very difficult to save the pet after he has been diagnosed with this disease. Mostly, it gets detected in later stages, so the treatment becomes all the more difficult.

Because the symptoms of this disease are very general, it is suggested that you ask your veterinarian to conduct yearly tests for your pet.

This would help in detecting any issue in the very beginning, which makes it possible to treat it successfully.

Avian Influenza

Monk Parakeets can contract avian influenza, and there is a possibility that they can transmit this illness to humans. Since 1997, the Centers for Disease Control and Prevention state that humans have contracted several different strains of the disease.

- While wild birds seldom die from the disease, avian influenza is often fatal to captive birds that often develop more virulent strains of the virus. Waterfowl seem to be especially susceptible to the disease.

- If you observe your Monk Parakeet breathing with the mouth open, there are chances that he is suffering from respiratory ailments. Other common signs of respiratory problems are sounds like wheezing or whistling when the Monk Parakeet is breathing.

- It is important to take care of respiratory problems at the earliest as they might be fatal to the Monk Parakeet. Monk Parakeets are also unable to function properly and carry out regular activities such as walking if they are unable to breathe properly.

- When Monk Parakeets become inactive, they also become severely stressed, leading to secondary problems like behaviour changes.

Remedy

One important thing that you must remember when you notice that your Monk Parakeet has respiratory problems is that you must consult your vet before taking any action. This is because problems related to the lungs of birds can be quite complex. Remember that the lungs of birds are modified or adapted to aid flying. As a result, the treatment of respiratory problems should be left to the specialists.

2. Taking care of a sick pet Monk Parakeet

If your Monk Parakeet is sick, then it is very important that you take him to a qualified veterinarian. It is never advised to self-medicate. For example, if your Monk Parakeet is suffering from fever and you decide to give the animal a medicine that you take for fever, then you are in for a shock.

The medicines that work on human beings or other animals might not necessarily work on your Monk Parakeet. You should never take this chance. Always consult the veterinarian before administering any medicine to the pet.

Along with the medication, you should also pamper the sick Monk Parakeet. Monk Parakeets love to be loved and pampered. You will see them recovering fast when you give them your attention and care.

While it will be a little difficult for you to take care of the Monk Parakeet when he is sick, the experience can actually strengthen the bond that you share with the pet Monk Parakeet.

The first sign that something is not right with the Monk Parakeet is the body temperature of the animal. He should ideally be around 70 degrees C. You should check this.

If you feel that the Monk Parakeet is very warm to the touch, then you should know that the pet is not well.

Other symptoms that can help you to know that the pet is unwell include a lazy and lethargic pet. If you feel that the pet is not himself and has been acting very lazily, then this could be because he is unwell.

The pads of the feet of the Monk Parakeet will also get warm in such a condition. This is another symptom that you should look out for.

When you see the symptoms of a high fever in the pet, the first thing that you should do is make sure that the pet is drinking water. He can be given Pedialyte to help him recover. You should consult a veterinarian if the temperature does not come down in a few hours.

It is very important that you don't ignore the health condition of the Monk Parakeet. Even if he has a slight fever, you should take it seriously because before you know the slight fever to take shape of a life threatening disease. So, never hesitate to consult a vet in case of any doubts.

After you have consulted the veterinarian, you will have to spend a lot of time with your pet while he is recuperating from his illness. This can get very daunting for a new owner because he would not want to commit a mistake while taking care of his beloved pet.

You can take some simple precautions to make sure that your pet is healing better and faster. These precautions will ensure that the pet is getting all that is required for his healing process.

To begin with, you should always make sure that the pet is warm and comfortable. The pet will require something to curl into. He will also need his privacy at this time. Make sure that the Monk Parakeet has a blanket or shirt that will allow him to do so.

Do not force him to do anything that he does not want to. The pet needs some time and space. You should allow him to rest for as long as he wants. This will help him to heal in a better way.

If you have more than one Monk Parakeet, then you need to keep the sick pet isolated. This is to give the ill pet time to get better and to avoid spreading the disease.

If there are things and toys that the pets share, you should wash these things nicely and keep them separately. You should wash the bedding and other washable accessories in the cage of the Monk Parakeet. A pet recovering surgery should be kept in a safe and closed environment so that he does not bruise himself.

A Monk Parakeet can get dehydrated very easily. The pet might throw up when he is not well. This can easily lead to dehydration. The Monk Parakeet will get disoriented if he is dehydrated for too long. You need to keep a check on the pet to ensure that he is not dehydrated.

You need to make sure that the pet is hydrated at all times. There is a simple way to find out whether the pet is dehydrated or not. You can pull the skin at the back of the neck of the Monk Parakeet. If the skin does not fall back easily, then the pet is definitely dehydrated.

You should make sure that the pet is drinking enough water to get better. But, in some cases the pet might just refuse to drink any water. The vet might also suggest intravenous injections in severe cases.

You should make sure that that the pet does not consume cold water. This can cause severe diarrhoea in the pet. Water at room temperature is the best for the Monk Parakeet.

If the Monk Parakeet is extremely dehydrated, you can serve him Pedialyte with water to help him get better. In severe cases, you can also give them Gatorade and water, but Gatorade needs to be diluted with larger quantities of water because of its high sugar content.

These fluids will help the Monk Parakeet to recover faster. Along with these mixes, your pet Monk Parakeet should have access to simple water at all times.

The veterinarian will suggest the exact dosage of the mixes that your Monk Parakeet needs depending on his condition. But, in general he should have 15-20 millilitres of the mix in every four hours.

A sick Monk Parakeet will get dehydrated pretty soon, so it is important to replenish his body with the water and the lost salts. If you feel that the pet is not having enough water, you should consult your vet about the condition of the pet.

If the pet Monk Parakeet does not drink the mix on his own, you will have to find a way to make him drink it. You can't force the pet, so the best way to replenish his body during a dehydration phase is to syringe feed him. If you take all the precautionary methods, this is not a difficult method.

To syringe feed the bird, take a clean syringe and fill it with the drink mix. Now, take this syringe to the side of the mouth of the pet. Slowly release a drop at a time in his mouth.

The Monk Parakeet will not be so easy to feed, so you need to be patient. You need to be careful so that the Monk Parakeet does not develop any infections.

The pet is not well, so you have to be prepared for making extra effort for him at this time. No matter how much the pet resists, you have to make sure that he is being well fed when he is recuperating. You should also make sure that the pet is taking a nutritious diet to allow his body to heal quickly.

A sick pet will also lose interest in eating his food. You might have to take out time and hand feed him. You can use canned food or baby food that is prescribed by the veterinarian.

It is important that the food is easy on his digestive system. The sick pet needs nutrition, but does not need the pressure of digesting heavy foods. If the food is difficult for the digestive system of the Monk Parakeet to break, it will lead to more complications.

Fixing a Broken Wing

The wings of Monk Parakeets form and important part of their defence mechanism and also help them maintain the balance of their bodies when they are running or walking upright. So, a broken wing is a serious issue that must be taken care of immediately.

Of course, you will require the assistance of a vet to help take care of the issue completely. However, first aid is necessary when you have a Monk Parakeet with a broken wing to ensure that the condition does not become worse.

There are several reasons why a Monk Parakeet might have a broken wing. If the bird becomes aggressive, they are capable of getting injured in fights. Mating among Monk Parakeets is so aggressive that, many times, the female might be attacked by several males at one time and actually breaks her wings.

In addition to this, an attack by a predator may also cause serious injuries to Monk Parakeets. There are always chances of the wing getting stuck in wires or mesh, leading to injuries like broken bones. Whatever the cause, broken wings can be very painful and must be take care of at the earliest possible opportunity.

A broken wing can cause excruciating pain and can lead to a lot of stress if left unattended. Sometimes, broken wings may also be accompanied by serious cuts and wounds that need to be treated properly to avoid infections. So it is necessary for you to be able to identify a broken wing.

When a wing is broken, it will hang very low. You will notice that it is displaced and is much lower than the other wing.

The first step to treating a broken wing is to gain the confidence of the bird to be able to handle it. Usually when they are injured, birds tend to become more defensive. Especially after an attack, a Monk Parakeet will not really be very easy to hold and take into your care.

First, give the Monk Parakeet some feed and also some water. If he actually begins to eat, it is much easier for you to get a grip on it. However, after a traumatizing injury, your Monk Parakeet is less likely to want to eat.

In such cases, the only option you have is to chase the Monk Parakeet to a corner and then catch it. You must be firm in your grip and must gently hold the wings down, taking great care with the broken wing.

The best way to calm a Monk Parakeet down is to set her in an isolated spot or even a small cage which is well lit and warm.

You must approach an injured Monk Parakeet only when you are certain that it has calmed down completely. Failing this, you will find yourself going through the entire process of calming it down again.

Gently examine the bird for wounds and cuts that might be bleeding. These wounds must be washed to remove any impurity that might lead to infection. The wound can be washed with some lukewarm water or even iodine solution. If you have an antiseptic that you have used before, you may apply it.

The next step is to provide a splint or support of the broken wing. You can use sticky gauze or even veterinary tape for this purpose. Hold the wing in the natural position first. It must be held against the body of the bird to make sure that it heals in its natural position.

Once the wing is in place, it needs to be bound to the body securely. Take the gauze or the tape around the body of the bird. The objective of the gauze and the tape is to ensure that the wing is immobilized. However, if you tie it too tightly, it might affect the breathing of the bird.

When you wrap the gauze, take it over the broken wing, around the body and under the wing that is functional. This will not restrict the movement of the other wing.

Usually, broken wings take about 4 weeks to heal completely. It is best that you keep the Monk Parakeet in a cage and in isolation until the wing is completely healed.

The quality of food must be very good during the healing period. Plenty of water must also be available for the bird to drink. In this period, if the gauze or tape becomes soiled, you may change it.

While you are changing the gauze, if you notice that the Monk Parakeet is able to move the wing comfortably, you can remove the dressing. If not, you can take the gauze off after four weeks. Now your bird is also ready to mingle with the rest of the flock and carry on with his routine.

If your bird has been attacked by a predator, he might require vaccinations or shots to ensure that there is no infection. Even in case of open wounds, it is best recommended that you have it checked by a professional.

Chapter 7: Maintaining the Monk Parakeet

When you decide to keep a Monk Parakeet as a pet, you should understand that you will have to pay attention to the basic cleaning and grooming of the Monk Parakeet. This is essential to keep the Monk Parakeet clean and healthy. Not only will your Monk Parakeet appear neat and clean, he will also be saved from many unwanted diseases.

When you are looking at grooming sessions for your Monk Parakeet, you should pay special attention to the Monk Parakeet's beaks, nails, wings and its bathing. This chapter will help you to understand the various dos and don'ts while grooming your pet Monk Parakeet.

A Monk Parakeet will be your companion for a very long time. You would also spend a lot of time with him on a daily basis. This only makes it imperative that you keep the bird in its best possible form. The bird should be pleasant and happy to look at. Who wants a messy kept pet at home?

1. Clipping the wings

A new pet parent of a Monk Parakeet will be faced with the dilemma of clipping its wings. If you too are in this stage then this section will help you to understand the significance of clipping and how to do it. This will help you to maintain your pet bird in a better way.

The time you clip the wings of the bird is very crucial. Your decision can affect the Monk Parakeet's future flights. It can also cause the Parakeet to have an accident. This means that you should know when to clip and how to clip to keep the Quaker Parrot safe and out of danger.

When a baby Quaker Parrot is getting weaned, you will see that the bird gets highly anxious and also gives up food to a great extent because it loses its appetite. In the natural surroundings, this is the time the baby slowly becomes independent and gives up the nest.

The bird will soon take its first flight. But, before the first fight can be taken, the chick should have good and developed breast muscles. The young bird needs to lose some weight for this to happen. It should also work on the young wings. The young chick loses over ten percent of weight at this time, but this helps him in taking that first flight.

The young chick will get back its appetite after the maiden flight. You can serve the chick good quality baby food to give him proper nutrition and energy. You should also let the pet have daily flights at this time and should also encourage him for exercise on a daily basis.

When the young bird gets proficient in flying, you should clip the wings of the chick. If the wings are clipped at a very early stage, the weaning period will be postponed. The chick will have to go through a lot of stress if this happens. It will get very difficult for the bird to carry on normal body functions at this time.

An early clipping of wings can create claustrophobic conditions for the Parrot. It can lose its sense of balance because of this. On the other hand, clipping the wings too late will make the bird irritated and resentful.

It is, therefore, very important that the time of clipping is absolutely proper. An early clipping and late clipping both are harmful for the overall well-being of the Monk Parakeet. Clipping the wings at the right time will keep the bird harmonious and in balance.

Clipping of a bird's wings is a very serious matter. You should always be careful about how you do it. If you are a novice, we will teach you how to go about it. But, in case of any doubts, it is always recommended that you consult a breeder or a veterinarian or a fellow pet parent who has experience in clipping the wings of a Parrot.

Clipping is a process that requires patience from your side. You have to slowly move from one feather to another. You have to change direction continuously. Sometimes, you move underneath and sometimes above. It requires you to be confident about your hand movements and also requires you to be slow and firm.

You need to start with the flight feathers. Trim the inverted patterns. This is called clipping inwards. You should be very careful with the Quaker at this stage. You don't want to hurt the pet in any way. If the pet tries to fly or if there is a strong wing, the bird can be seriously injured. So, make sure that you are holding the bird in a way that your work gets done but you don't hurt the pet bird.

You need to trim the quill base of the Monk Parakeet as finely as possible. After having done so, you can move upward towards the primaries. You need to be soft and slow so that the bird is not hurt in the process. The shaft stub should be hidden manually under the covert of the bird like an envelope.

You should extend the bird's wings by the tips in a very delicate fashion. You should use sharp scissors that are bird clawed and have round edges. You have to be extremely careful that you don't touch the blood feather. You can't cut it.

Each bird is different. The kind of flight that they take also defines them. A light and strong flying bird requires you to cut a couple of extra feathers on the wings. You should observe the landing of the bird when it flies to know what kind of a flyer the bird is. Another thing that needs to be noted here is the all the primary and secondary wings of the bird should never be cut.

2. Trimming claws of the Monk Parakeet

The only way you can trim the claws of the Monk Parakeet is by making him comfortable with you. The pet bird can be very restless. He will get away from your grip, in turn hurting itself. So, the first step is to bond well with the pet.

It is important to cut the nails of the Monk Parakeets regularly. You should be looking at doing so at least once a month. If the nails of the Monk Parakeet are not cut on a regular basis, there is a chance that the nails will get stuck somewhere. This will cause the nails to get uprooted.

You can imagine the pain your Monk Parakeet will have to go through if the nails are uprooted. You will have to rush to the veterinarian to help the Monk Parakeet. Not only this, the long nails can also leave marks and scratches on your skin. So, make it a point to cut the nails of the pet regularly.

You should also make sure that you use the right equipment to cut the nails of the pet Monk Parakeet. You should use good quality animal nail clippers. Along with that, you would need soap and styptic powder.

You can begin with giving a treat to the Monk Parakeet. This is to distract the animal so that he does not disturb you when you are busy clipping his nails.

If there is someone else in the house, you can ask them to hold the Monk Parakeet. This will make your job easier. But, even if there is no one, you can do it on your own. Place the Monk Parakeet in your lap in a way that he is comfortable and you have access to his nails.

You will notice a reddish vein on the nail. You should cut the nail in a way that the vein is not touched. If you happen to hurt it, it will hurt the pet and will also bleed.

In case, you cut a nail in way that the vein starts bleeding, use the soap to clean it and then apply the powder. This will give relief to the pet. You should give a few minutes to the Monk Parakeet to feel better before starting the process of clipping the nails once again.

3. Trimming the beak of the Monk Parakeet

Most species of Parrots are capable of trimming their own beaks by the process of chewing. But, at times, due to malnutrition, illness, chewing on certain toys, a Monk Parakeet can overgrow the break, which you will have to trim because an overgrown beak can cause pain to the Parrot.

Keep a check on the bird's beak to notice if it needs trimming. If improper trimming is done, it can be a cause of great misery to the bird. You have the option of visiting an avian doctor. He will trim the beak as per requirement.

Only an experienced person should do the trimming of the Monk's beak because it is a very delicate procedure. The bird needs to be restrained with the help of gloved hands.

The top part of the beak will have to be tucked in the other half. The person can start trimming at this time. Trimming should be done till white spots are visible. Don't go beyond because that will hurt the Monk Parakeet.

The key here is that the biting surface should be levelled. If it is distorted, the bird will face issues while chewing food and holding stuff. Before starting the process, the bird's beak needs to be cleaned properly with a disinfectant. A fresh head should be used on the grinding tool to eliminate chances of any infection.

The bird's beak may remain sore for a few days after trimming. It is important that you give time to the bird to recover. Serve only soft foods such as sprouted seeds, soft fruits and vegetables at this time so that the bird is not required to chew much on the food.

4. Bathing the Parakeet

Nobody wants to have a dirty pet. It is your responsibility that the pet is maintained at all times. A simple bath is one such routine that you can follow with your Parakeet to make sure that he is neat and clean.

You will be thrilled to know here that it is not difficult to bathe a Parakeet. In fact, It is known that Monk Parakeets love to take a bath. Unlike many pets, you will have no issues bathing your pet Parrot.

To start with, you need a small dish or a small basin. If you leave the pet near this water dish, the pet will take a bath on its own because the Monk Parakeets are fond of taking water splashes. You can let the pet do this himself or herself.

You can also lightly spray water over the Parrot with a bottle every day. A daily misting is considered good for the Monk Parakeet. Some Parrots might not enjoy misting or spraying of water. You will have to spray and check whether your Monk Parakeet is up for it or not.

If you want to be sure and want to take matters in your own hands, then you can bathe the pet on your own.

The bird needs to be bathed regularly to remove all the dirt. The dirt on the skin and the feathers will loosen because of contact with water. The Quaker also displays preening, where that feathers will become waterproof to some degree. Bathing on a regular basis also helps the pet to get rid of dry and itchy skin.

When you are looking to give a nice bath to your Monk Parakeet, you should be looking at two things, a good quality mild shampoo and a few towels. It is very important that you choose the right shampoo for the Monk Parakeet.

If the shampoo is too hard or harsh, it will leave rashes on the Monk Parakeet and might even cause serious damage to his skin.

You can buy a good quality cat shampoo or a baby shampoo for the Monk Parakeet. These shampoos are very mild on the skin and have proven to be ideal for a Monk Parakeet. You also need a few towels handy for the Monk Parakeet. While one will be used to dry the water off, the others are required to cover the ground or floor.

Another way to bathe your naughty Monk Parakeet is to sway him under running warm water. Turn the tap on and make sure the water is warm. It should not be cold or too hot. Once you are convinced that the temperature of the water is right for the pet, hold the pet and bring him under the water for a few seconds.

Before he starts to get fidgety, take him away from the water. Now apply some shampoo over the Monk Parakeet. Keeping swaying him under the water till all the shampoo is washed off.

It is very important that all the shampoo is washed off; else the Monk Parakeet's skin will be affected and will show signs of rashes and abrasions.

While you are bathing the Monk Parakeet, it is important that you protect his face. Water should not enter his eyes or ears. These are sensitive areas and water could cause some damage to them.

Keep him on the towels and use another towel to pat him dry. Make sure that he is absolutely dry before you let him go, otherwise he will stick dust and dirt on his skin.

After the bath is done, place the Monk Parakeet in a big towel. You should place a few blankets or towels on the floor to keep it warm and tight for the Monk Parakeet. The Monk Parakeet will show too much energy at this time. He will try to escape you. You should be very gentle with the pet, otherwise you could harm him.

5. Giving the pet adequate exercise

Maintenance of the Monk Parakeet also means that you have to make efforts to maintain the physical and mental health of the Parakeet. Adequate exercise will play a very important role in maintenance of both the physical and mental health.

In the natural surroundings, the Monk Parakeet has a very active wild life. Even if the bird eats high calorie fatty seeds, it maintains its health because of flying here and there all the time. A captive bird in a cage has a very different lifestyle. This needs to be kept in mind while raising a pet bird.

The bird has to fly for miles in the wild to acquire food on a daily basis. This keeps the bird fit and fine. No matter how much you try, you can never give the pet the same environment that it would have gotten in the wild. You can't emulate a system where a pet bird can fly for miles.

In a home environment, a bird can't be made to fly for miles. Some people chip the wings of the bird so that he does not fly away. This makes it all the more difficult. The bird has to exercise. This is a fact. You will have to find out ways to do so.

Not many people know that even Parakeets can suffer from obesity. If the bird does not move enough, the bird will pile up fat which will lead to many other issues, such as diabetes and circulatory issues. To rule out all these problems, you need to make sure that the bird exercises.

If you have any doubt, you should always consult a veterinarian. This section will help you to understand how you can help your pet Parakeet to exercise to stay fit, physically and mentally.

But, if you are not convinced with how you should go about this, it is advised that you consult a veterinarian and discuss with him the various types of exercises your pet can do.

The vet will help you to choose the best possible exercise routine for your Parrot. You should make sure that you include exercise in his daily life. This section will help you to understand how you can do so in your daily life.

You can easily get some equipment to exercise either from online retailers or from a pet store nearby. You can also talk to other pet parents about which

Parrot exercises they prefer. This will help you to make an exercise schedule for your pet Parakeet.

To utilise the high energy of the pet Parrot, you can use toys as a simple way to engage him. You can buy special ropes, bells, bongs and swings for the pet Parakeet. These equipment can be used by the Parrot to hang, swing and flap around. This will allow the pet to utilise the energy in a good way.

There are handheld rope toys easily available on the market. The pet can hang on the rope, while you swing him back and forth. You can engage the pet by talking to him. If the pet enjoys the rope, he will start flapping his wings, thus giving him a good workout.

Wing drumming is also known to be a very good exercise form for the pet Parrot. When a Parrot is taken out the cage in the morning after spending the night in the cage, you will notice that he stands at the edge and drums his wings fiercely. This is good for him. Make sure that you are around at this time so that you can control if something goes wrong.

The bird can be encouraged to move up and down a hanging rope. This will engage him and will help him utilise his high energies. Such ropes are safe for the pet. You or any other family member should be around when the bird is playing such games.

You can also engage the pet in a shower with warm water every day. You might be surprised but this will also help the bird to get some exercise. The bird will excitedly flap his wings when hit with warm water. He will hop around excitedly, hence getting some exercise.

It is also known that the quality of a Monk Parakeet's feathers improves if it is swathed in warm water every day. A simple warm water shower can keep the pet bird healthy and also clean.

You can also get a paper ball for the pet. The ball is safe for him and will help him to use his high energies. The pet Parrot can also be seen tossing and turning all around with the ball.

He will get very happy and busy with such a ball. Allow him to play with the ball for as long as he enjoys it. Do this every day.

Chapter 8: Training the Monk Parakeet

It is very important to train the pet to make him more suitable to a household. By nature, Monk Parakeets can be a little naughty. You will have to train them to extract the best from them.

You would definitely want the pet to be well trained. Though the Monk Parakeet has been domesticated since ages, but you have to train him for making him more suitable to your home.

Most people prefer Parrots as pets because of their ability to talk and entertain. These birds are fun to be around. You and your family can have a great time if you have a Quaker Parrot as a pet.

It should be noted here that you will have to spend some time and energy in training and grooming the pet if you wish to extract the best from the Monk Parakeet. The training will allow you to get the best Quaker behaviour and the grooming will allow you to keep the pet healthy and clean.

1. Training the pet

The pet needs to trust you if you want to train it effectively. Once the Parakeet is comfortable with you and your family, things will only get simpler for you. So, the first and foremost task is to establish trust with the pet Parrot.

There are a few points that need to be kept in mind when you are training your pet Quaker bird. The following points will help you to understand the dos' and don'ts of this journey with the pet Quaker bird:

- It is important that you understand the motivation behind your pet's behaviour. It is important to understand that the Parrots will also have a reason to do what they do. If they are biting you, there should be a reason behind it. So, you need to understand the reason behind each action.

- If the Parrot is not behaving well, you need to take responsibility. The bird is very social and can be taught to behave in the best possible way by the pet-owner.

- The bird will not respond to threats or punishments. So, if you are thinking of punishing the bird to train it your way, then you will not be successful. You should focus on ways to reward the bird so that the bird remains motivated.

- The best way to teach the bird is to reward all the good things it does and to just ignore the things that shouldn't have been done. This will teach the bird what you approve and what you don't. You can also be a little firm at times but refrain from the practice of punishing the bird. This will not help you or the bird in any way.

2. Teaching the Quaker to talk

Most people think that all Parrots can easily mimic human sounds and effortlessly talk. But, this is not true. A young Parrot can be trained to talk. But, all the species of the pet bird are not good in imitating human sounds.

If you wish your Quaker bird to talk then you need to invest in a lot of energy and time on the bird. You should know that it will not be as easy as you think. You need to be dedicated and patient if you wish to see your bird successfully imitating sounds and talking.

It is important that you treat the young bird as a small child. Like a small child needs to be taught everything, your Quaker bird will also need to learn from you. The bird has no vocabulary of its own to fall back on.

You might have a very difficult time teaching the bird the very first word. But, if you don't give up and keep at it, you will soon be surprised to see how fast the bird is learning.

The bird has a good observation power and is also a quick learner. This makes it simpler for the pet-owner to train them. They can be taught to talk and imitate human sounds. You need to keep repeating a certain action if you want the bird to pick up that action. So, if you want the bird to learn a word, you need to keep repeating the word in front of the Quaker bird.

Teach the bird the way you would approach a child, but you need to avoid childlike intonation. You should use simple words to describe various things to the Monk Parakeet. You should start this process from the very first day. You need to talk to the bird like you are having a conversation with him. This is a way to make the bird follow you.

If you follow the guidelines given in this section, you will realise that training the pet to talk and to do other tasks can actually be a lot of fun. The key is to know what needs to be done and what needs to be avoided at all costs.

Timetable

Often people get too excited when they get a pet home, especially a pet such as a Monk Parakeet. They wish to teach the Parrot everything in one go. This will never work, so you should refrain from such practices.

In their natural surroundings, a young Quaker will learn vocalisations from his parents. When you take away the natural surroundings from an animal, you need to bear the brunt of it. You will have to function as the parent of the pet.

A young pet might show a lot of enthusiasm in the beginning. You might see your pet picking up phrases very fast. But, do not get over excited and don't overdo things. Keep them as simple as possible.

It is always advised to start from simple words such as 'hello', 'hi', 'up'. Practice perseverance and patience. Give your pet a lot of time and space to learn. It is better to be slow and steady, instead of starting out with vigour and then losing out in the middle.

Quaker Parrots can surprise you. There have been instances when the pet owner was on the verge of giving up, the Quaker surprised the pet owner by starting to speak fluently. There are few Quakers that might take weeks and some that might take years. You need to understand that each Quaker will be different from the other.

You will have a unique experience. But, one thing is for sure that if you don't give up the Quaker will learn to speak sooner or later. Just keep going and never force the pet with anything that you want him to do.

Importance of interaction

As you go along the road of training your Quaker Parrot, you will understand the importance of interacting with the bird. It needs to be understood here that if your pet is taking an unusual amount of time to learn, you need to spend more time with the pet. This is the key to form a good relation with your bird.

A Quaker bird is known to be a flock bird. It enjoys being in a flock. These Quakers use various techniques to impress and to grab the attention of other flock members. When the bird is away from its natural surroundings and is in your home, you are its flock member.

The pet Quaker will readily take to speaking and will show more interest when it will learn that it can communicate with a flock member, which is you in this case, with the help of these words. That trust needs to be developed that both of you belong to the same flock.

If you understand how a Quaker bird functions in real life, everything will fall into place. You will find it extremely easy to teach the pet and to communicate with it. The bird needs your attention and you need to show the Quaker that you are there for him.

A Quaker bird is similar to a young kid. The kid needs the right stimulation and correct responses to help him learn. And, above all he needs patience and love. Your Quaker also needs the same things. The bird needs to be encouraged so that it can perform better and learn better.

If you think that you can keep one hour each day for the pet and then expect the Quaker to learn everything in one week, it obviously won't work. You will only be miserable and in turn the pet will also be miserable. You will learn along the way, but be prepared to take the process with lots of genuine love for the Quaker bird. This will work more than anything else.

3. Methods of training

As a pet parent of the Quaker, you might be wondering how to about to go about this training process. This section will help you to learn more and adopt the right methods to teach your pet to pick up words, phrases and sounds.

The words that you use throughout the day, will easily be picked up. You and your family should spend a lot of time around the bird. This will give the bird a lot of time to catch words and phrases.

If a phone is in the vicinity of the Quaker, every time the phone rings and someone says a hello, the bird will register. Before you know it your Quaker will start saying the word hello. This is how the bird tries to imitate and also be a part of the flock or family.

The Quaker will actually surprise you by its imitating skills. The bird will pick up some unusual sounds that are repeated around him. If the bird is kept near the balcony, the bird will pick up sounds of horns of cars. If the bird is kept near the kitchen, the Quaker will pick up sounds such as the whistle of the cooker.

A training method that is very popular with many people that have Parrots is usage of talking CDs. These are easily available online. These CDs allow the pet to improve on expressions that he has already learnt. They might not be great for parodying.

The best way to train your pet will also be effective interaction with the pet. The interaction needs to be extensive and intensive. The bird should learn to talk not as a task or punishment but as an extended part of his social behaviour. You will notice how much effort the bird puts in to impress you and to feel a part of the family. It will repeat phrases that it learns so that it can attract your attention.

Another training method is the association method. Association means when you associate your words with an emotion or with an object. This method allows the bird to learn via responses which works great for them. You need to label stuff with words when you interact with your pet Quaker. This labelling will help the Quaker bird to learn faster in a better way.

You have to be clear and loud if you wish your pet to be able to follow you. You can't expect the poor animal to imitate you if he is not able to get you clear. You should stress on each syllable while speaking. This will allow the pet Parrot to catch you in a better way and hence imitate you in a better way.

It is also important to use the right kind of words around the Parrot. The entire family should be aware of the fact that if the Monk Parakeet can catch your other words, he can also catch the foul language that you might use. You should not use any bad words in the vicinity of the Parakeet.

The more excited you are, the more enthusiastic the Monk Parakeet will get. It is as simple as that. If you are dull in your training sessions, this is what you can expect from the bird. The more chirpy and clear you are, the better the Monk Parakeet will follow you.

The Parrot has less intentions of having a good conversation and more of impressing you. It wants you to notice him and laud him. It will work harder and do better just to capture that attention of yours.

You can employ some simple tools when you are training your Quaker Parrot. These tools are as follows:

- **Repetition**: Repetition is definitely the key for training a Quaker Parrot well. The more the number of times a Parrot listens to a word, the better the chances of it picking up the word. You and your family should try to repeat the words that you wish the Parrot to learn. Give the Parrot some time and you will be surprised as to how quickly he learns what you intended him to learn. The Parrot assumes that the words and sentences being repeated are important and he needs to know them to be a part of the flock or the family. Hence, the bird reflects this in his actions by learning those words and sentences.

- **Association**: Association means when you associate your words with an emotion or with an object. This method allows the bird to learn via responses which works great for them. You need to label stuff with words when you interact with your pet Quaker. You can also associate good work with certain treats. If the Parrot does something right, you can treat him with the food of his choice. When you repeatedly do something like this, the Quaker will know that he will be rewarded when you are happy with his actions.

- **Spontaneous speech**: It has also been noticed that the bird will pick up things from your everyday speech. You can place the T perch of the bird in the living area or in an area that is frequented by the family members all the time. This will allow the Parrot to be part of spontaneous speeches. This will help the Quaker to learn. Never keep the pet isolated. This will affect his learning curve. He needs to hear, pick up and then practice, and for this to happen he needs people around him.

Training sessions

A training session is best effective if the trainee is responding well to the training being offered. You have to constantly look for signals that your Monk Parakeet is taking well to the training sessions that are being held for him.

To begin with, try to keep the sessions at times when you know that the Quaker is very energetic. You should also keep the sessions at the same time every day. This allows the Quaker to look forward to his learning session every day.

There are some body reactions of the Quaker Parrot that will help you to understand that he is learning well. You should look out for these body reactions in the Quaker Parrot. You will notice that the Parrot stares at you intently and with a great focus. You will also notice his pupils changing as and when you speak. When you notice such responses, you should know that this is the best time to teach your Parakeet.

It is also important to be able to hold your Parrot's interest. The last thing that you want is to lose your Parrot's attention. You should always start with simple words and syllables. Never put too much pressure on the poor fellow in the very beginning. You need to be slow and steady. It is the only way to win this particular race.

All Quakers are different. Take some time to understand your bird. Give him as much time as he needs to learn. You should remember that if you are bored, the Parrot will be bored. It is important that you keep your spirits high if you want the Parrot to show you significant improvement.

If you are looking for some tips to make the road ahead simpler and also fun for you then the following tips will help you a lot:

- The Monk Parakeets are known to be very alert during the mornings. You can choose this time every day to talk to the bird and teach the bird. The bird has to be responsive, so it is always best to choose a time when the Parrot is most expressive, which is generally the morning time.

- Some people believe that teaching the bird for two hours will yield great results. This is not true. While it will be great if you can spend two hours with the bird, the training session should not last more than 30 minutes. The most ideal and effective training session will be 15-20 minutes. You will see great results if you follow this simple tip.

- Never confuse the bird. Some people think that they can teach the Monk everything in a couple of sittings. It never works like that. You need to be patient. Take up a single word or phrase. Repeat it many times and then go to the next one. The next day, start with the previous day's words and phrases.

- When the bird is taught too much in less time, he does not get the chance to replicate your voice well.

- He needs to understand and control the tonality of the words that he attempts. It is important to give him time to be able to do so.

- The bird might learn too many words at one time, but he will not be able to imitate your voice. The bird might just mumble incoherently if it is forced to learn too much in one go.

- Be prepared with what you want to teach the bird. Come up with a creative way that helps the bird to associate your actions and words. Keep repeating things that are working.

- You should always remember that the Parakeet is trying as hard as you are trying. Don't assume that it is only you who is doing all the hard work. An understanding that both of you are working hard will allow you to give the Monk Parakeet some space and time.

- You should keep away the things that would distract the Parakeet during the training sessions. For example, you can keep the toys of the Parrot away so that the bird can focus on you and the training session being done.

- You should make use of similar phrases for related tasks. For example, the word 'want' can be used when the bird wishes to have food or water. 'Want some grapes', want some water'. This will help the bird to associate want with food and water.

- You should be as involved as one can be. This will help you to learn a lot. You don't want to make the sessions about a strict teacher student relationship. It has to be more of a two way road.

- You should always try to make associations interesting for the Monk Parakeet.

- If you wish to see the bird showing overall development, you need to include things from his environment also. For example, every time there is a specific background noise, you should address it for the bird.

- Never deprive the Parakeet of food to speed up his learning process. This will never work. The Quaker will not be able to understand the logic behind all this. The bird might fall ill because of the deprivation of food, but it will definitely not learn a thing.

4. Training for responsive conversation

While you will enjoy your bird repeating words and phrases at random times, it can get boring after a while. No conversation is fun if it is only one way. You will have to train the bird to have a responsive conversation. This will be more fun for both you and the Parrot.

But, you should remember here that teaching the Parrot to imitate words, sentences, voices and other sounds around him is in itself a task, teaching him to indulge in a two way conversation is another uphill task. As the pet parent, you have the right to decide where you want to stop the training of the Parrot.

If you have decided that you want the responsive conversation to be a part of the Monk Parakeet's training, then you will have to include some more tips and tricks in your regular training sessions with the Parakeet.

You should prepare a list of questions and answers that you want to include in your training session. It should be noted here that you need to prepare both the questions and the answers. For example, to a question "do you want grapes?", you can prepare the answer "yes".

When you are training the pet, after the daily dose of repetition of words and phrases, you should start with your list of questions and answers. Whisper the question to the Parrot in a very soft voice.

After that, answer to that question in a loud and expressive voice. This technique will help the Monk Parakeet to differentiate between a question and an answer.

When you keep the question low key and the answer high pitched, the Quaker will automatically pay attention to the answer. It will associate that answer with the low key question that is being repeated with it. If you keep repeating this system, the Parakeet will soon start answering the questions that you ask him.

Quaker Parrots are intelligent, so they will grasp more than you intend to teach them. If you are patient and consistent in your practice with the bird, you will notice that the bird will slowly form a vocabulary bank.

Clicker training

A clicker is a small device that can be used for training your Monk Parakeet. It makes a sound that can communicate to a pet that a certain action needs to be done and that he will be suitably rewarded for the same. This helps the pet to understand why he is getting the treat that he is receiving.

Clicker training can help you to save time as it tries to make a link between a good response and also its reward and reinforcement. It can be successfully used to teach new behaviour to the pet with the help of its voluntary and natural behaviours.

You also need to condition the clicker. This means that you need to attach the click sound to a treat that the pet enjoys. You can select a treat that the pet is very fond of. It is also advised that such training sessions should happen before the pet has its food. If the pet has no appetite, it might not be motivated enough to work hard for a treat.

5. Target training

Target training is also very popular with the pet parents of the Quaker Parrots. This allows you to teach the bird to touch a thing or item with the help of a gentle grab or with the help of an open beak. Once the bird is comfortable doing this, you can further treat him to follow a target before grabbing it.

Simple things such as a toy, or chopstick can be used as a target. You can eventually train the bird to associate a command to this action so that when the bird listens to the command, it knows that it has to chase a target.

The target can be used as the main cue in this type of training. The target can be of any shape and size. You should not worry about this. Just make sure that the target object is not toxic to the Parakeet. Otherwise, this can be fatal to the health of the pet Parrot.

You can start from the T stand. Keep the target in from of the Parrot near the stand. By your movements and gestures encourage your pet to move towards the target. You can keep a treat in the other hand so that the pet Parrot gets motivated to get the treat. You can also use the click training here and make use of the clicker to guide the Monk Parakeet.

You should repeat this exercise many times each day. Move the target up and down to test the pet's focus. You should encourage the pet to grab the target gently and not fiercely.

This can be easily done by offering the treat to the pet Parrot only when he gently grasps the target. This will teach him that he gets the treat only when he grabs the object gently.

Keep the training process as simple as possible. Too much complication will only confuse your Monk Parakeet and in the end, it will end up learning nothing. This is something you would never want.

Once the pet Parrot is comfortable with getting to the target kept near the T stand, you can take the training session at a different spot. You should change the target object also. This will prepare the Monk Parakeet for different situations and different targets.

6. Trick training

If you are a person who wants his pet to perform various acrobats, then you are in for luck here. The Monk Parakeet is a bird that can be taught some simple tricks. You can teach the tricks to the pet and enjoy the family loving Parrot performing those tricks.

You can also show off in front of people who come to your house. The Parrot will make sure that it entertains people with his tricks. This section will explain some basic tricks that can be easily taught to the Parrot with some patience and consistence.

Perching on T- stand

A very simple trick that can be taught to the bird is the perching trick. You can make the bird perch on its T stand. You can make it perch on your hand or arm and then back to the T stand.

Start when the bird is already on the T stand. Offer him some sunflower seeds or other foods that it likes. Gently say the words "come" and offer him your arm.

The bird will land itself on your arm. After that you can repeat the same process to make it perch on the T stand.

After this simple activity has been repeated many times, you will see that the bird takes less amount of time and follows your instructions easily. You should also encourage the Monk Parakeet by saying "good" each time it successfully perches.

Shaking hands

You can also make your Parrot bird shake hands. This is one of the most popular tricks of all Parrot parents. People love showing off such birds that can easily do such tricks.

The bird should be sitting on the T stand. At this time, tender the right hand. The bird will try to touch your right hand with its left foot. You should stop at this time.

Just remove your hand at this time. The idea is that the bird needs to learn to step on your right hand with his right foot and not the left. This will take some time. But, you should not give up and keep trying.

You will observe as you keep repeating the task and keep removing your hand, the bird will soon learn that something else needs to be done. It will replace its left foot with the right one eventually. You should not forget to give the bird a reward at this time.

You should also take care that the bird does not put all its body weight on your hand. It should be encouraged not to do so.

You should show by your physical actions that you don't approve the bird putting so much weight on your hand. The Parrot will definitely learn eventually.

Wave

You can also successfully teach the Monk Parakeet to wave. This is one of the most popular tricks of all Parrot parents.

The bird should be sitting on the T stand. At this time, tender the right hand. Now start wiggling your fingers. It should look like you are trying to create a wave.

You should also attach some verbal cue to the sign that you are doing. Keep saying "wave" loud and clear while making the wave.

Now, put the hand in front of the Parrot as a gesture to let him sit on the hand. When the bird lifts its foot to perch on your hand, remove your hand. This will send an indication to the bird that something else needs to be done.

Keep repeating these actions and soon your bird will start raising its foot as soon as you say the word "wave". The bird should be able to raise its foot very high and then drop it slowly.

When the bird does it, give him a treat. He will understand that this needs to be done. This is the start of the wave.

You should keep repeating the activity to get a foot. It is important that the bird lifts and lowers the leg voluntarily. Don't force it to do so. Don't get brutal with the poor bird. Just have patience and train the bird well.

Retrieving objects

This might come as a surprise to many people but your bird can also be taught to retrieve objects. This is a complicated task so it will take longer for the bird to be able to do so, but if you keep trying, you will surely succeed. The key is to be patient and to not give up.

Retrieving objects is a behaviour pattern that can be taught to the Monk Parakeet. The Parakeet is a bird that is always ready to learn new patterns from people it likes. This stimulates them in a very positive way. So, you should always go ahead and teach them new things.

You should always start from simple tricks. When the bird has mastered the simpler ones, you can move on to more complex ones. Retrieving an object is a simple trick that can be easily taught to the pet Parakeet.

Give the pet some time to understand and learn the technique and then you enjoy when he performs for you, your friends and family.

The bird should be sitting on the T stand. This will ensure that the bird does not wander away when the training is underway. At this time, take a heavy but small object and place in the middle of your hand. Take your hand forward and place it in front of the Monk Parakeet.

Most probably, the Parrot will pick up the object from your palm with the help of its beak. If the bird does not pick up the object even after repeated tries then you need to alter the strategy.

You can keep a small food item that the pet enjoys and keep it in the middle of your palm. The Monk Parakeet will definitely pick up the food item.

Repeat this with the object now. You can also use verbal cues such as "pick" or a clicker to give a signal to the pet. He will understand that he is supposed to used his beak and pick up the object when you give a cue.

After the Monk Parakeet is comfortable picking up the object, you can make it drop the object also. Keep a bowl below the T stand and signal the pet to drop by giving the cue "drop". When the pet drops it, give him a treat or motivate him with good words such as "good" or "well done".

You can keeping moving the bowl and each time the Parrot missed the bowl, don't give him the treat and ask him to do it again. This way he will understand that he needs to pick up objects and then throw them only in the bowl.

The marble and cup technique

The marble and cup is a very popular and interesting game that can be taught to the Monk Parakeet. The bird might take some time to get used to it, but once the bird is adept, you will be amazed by all that the bird can do.

You can also show off in front of people who come to your house. The Parrot will make sure that it entertains people with his tricks.

You should start by making sure that the bird is in a comfortable position. It should be watching you. You can make it perch on the T stand. Get three cups and place them over a table.

Now get a small ball or a small marble and put the ball or marble in one of these cups. You should overturn all the cups at this point.

The bird should be really interested in what's happening and should have his eyes glued at the balls and the table. Now, slowly move all the three cups. Bring the bird on the table. Encourage him to walk upto the overturned cups.

You should turn the cup with the ball or marble. The bird will slowly understand that the game is about finding the cup with the ball.

To make the Parrot understand this game, you can make a mark on one of the cups. Make sure that you use a colour that stands out. You should now tap the top of the cup to gain the attention of the Parakeet towards the mark that you have made.

You can keep a few seeds on the mark to make the pet move towards the marked cup. You can also slightly tap or scratch on the head of the Parrot to make it move.

This type of training will anyways take time, so don't rush. Even if you are stuck at a place, don't give up. Give slow and keep moving in the right direction. This is the only way to get things done from the Monk Parakeet.

Once the pet understands that it needs to move towards the marked cup, it will start doing it even if you give him a slight nod or some other indication. This is first phase of the training. Keep repeating these actions and once you are successful, you should move to the next phase.

In the next phase of the training, the pet will have to knock out the overturned cup that has the visible mark. Make the pet move towards the cup and then knock out the cup with your hands. Do this every time the pet moves towards the marked cup.

Slowly, the pet will start understanding that the marked cup also needs to be knocked out. He will take charge and will start doing it on his own after a few times. Keep repeating these actions to make the pet more comfortable doing the task.

Once the pet has learnt what needs to be done, you can start keeping the ball or marble in the marked cup. You should make sure that the mark is very small so that other people can't see it, but the pet should be able to make it out.

The pet is now ready to perform this game in front of other people. The people will be amazed how the pet will move towards the three cups and knock out the one that has the ball or the marble.

The trick will make your pet very popular, of course the real trick will be between you and your beloved pet.

7. Litter training

The Monk Parakeet will not automatically know where to litter. It will do it anywhere if it has to. If you see it from the bird's point of view, then it is used to doing so in its natural habitat. If you want your pet to be litter trained, then it is you who has to litter train him.

The last thing a person wants is poop all over him or his family members. There are a few people who believe that litter training a Monk Parakeet is very difficult. But, the reality is that it is perfect doable. You too can train your Parrot with some efforts from your side.

First, you need to pick a stimulus. This will act as the toilet for the Monk. This stimulus can be anything from a rag bag to a small bin. Next take out the bird from the cage on your hand. Slowly take him towards the bin.

Now, you need to give clues to the pet that you want him to litter in the bin. You can come up with creative ways to do so. You should also use some verbal indication such as "potty" along with the action that you are showing. The pet will slowly learn that you are asking him to do potty in the bin.

You should keep a check on the schedule of the pet. Does he defecate after food? or in the morning? When you are able to find a time when the pet does so, take him out of the cage and take him towards the bin.

Make him understand that you want him to defecate in the bin. When the urge gets strong, the pet will litter in the litter bin.

If you want to take things to the next level, you can also teach the bird to fly towards the bin when it needs to defecate. This can only be done if the wings of the Monk Parakeet are not clipped. You need to direct him to fly towards the bin. You should always use the same command to instruct the pet to defecate. This will keep things simpler for the Monk Parakeet and you also.

You should understand that an older bird will take a lot of time to get trained in this department. This is because he is used to a way of his own and he will require some time to understand what you want out of him.

This is precisely the reason why it is urged that you train the pet in an early stage. An infant can pick up these commands easily as compared to an older bird. But, in any case you need to be patient and calm during the entire process.

8. Some tips and tricks

It is always advised that you should start training sessions with an infant Monk Parakeet. This will help you to understand the pet well and will also give the pet some time to understand you and your training style.

Having said that, you can start at any age. If the pet is older, that does not mean that you can't train the pet now. You can definitely train the pet at a later stage also. You just need to be more patient with your sessions.

Because your Monk Parakeet is very intelligent, you also need to be smart with him. You need to adopt various tricks to keep the pet entertained and also to train him well. You will learn of some such tricks in this section.

- You should react with a visual nod when you approve of something the pet does. This will encourage the pet to give his best.
- You should never delay your pet Parakeet's reward. If the pet deserves a treat, it needs to be given immediately.
- If you delay it, you will only confuse the pet as to why he is getting the treat. The association process will get delayed.
- You have to know how much repetitions of a certain task is needed. You don't want to bore the Quaker Parrot and you also don't want to leave a task midway.
- Look for visible changes in the mood of the Parrot. Change the task when you see the bird getting disinterested.
- You should always start the training with the pet Parrot's natural abilities. These include tasks such as wings up, wave and lying on back.
- After you have tapped the natural abilities of the Monk Parakeet, you should move on to other type of trainings.
- The training sessions need not be strict or very intense. You should be able to enjoy all the right and wrong things the pet does. You should also let the pet experience your fun side.
- Don't make the session time a time of hell for the pet.
- You should never lose your cool on the pet. It is okay if the pet does not learn any tricks because in the end they are only tricks for some fun.

- There is no need to make the life of your pet hell for making him learn something for your amusement.

Conclusion

Thank you again for purchasing this book!

I hope this book was able to help you in understanding the various ways to domesticate and care for Monk Parakeets.

Monk Parakeets are adorable and lovable animals. These animals have been domesticated from many years. Even though they are loved as pets, they are not very common, and there are still many doubts regarding their domestications methods and techniques. There are many things that the prospective owners don't understand about the animal. They find themselves getting confused as to what should be done and what should be avoided.

If you are still contemplating whether you want to domesticate the Monk Parakeet or not, then it becomes all the more important for you to understand everything regarding the pet very well. When you are planning to domesticate a Monk Parakeet as a pet, you should lay special emphasis on learning about its behaviour, habitat requirements, diet requirements and common health issues.

The ways and strategies discussed in the book are meant to help you get acquainted with everything that you need to know about Monk Parakeets. You will be able to understand the unique antics of the animal. This will help you to decide whether the Monk Parakeet is suitable to be your pet. The book teaches you simple ways that will help you to understand your pet. This will allow you take care of your pet in a better way. You should be able to appreciate your pet and also care well for the animal with the help of the techniques discussed in this book.

Thank you and good luck!

References

Note: at the time of printing, all the websites below were working. As the internet changes rapidly, some sites might no longer be live when you read this book. That is, of course, out of our control.

www.ehow.co.uk

https://www.lovethatpet.com

http://www.Parrotsecrets.com

https://www.thespruce.com

https://www.bluecross.org.uk

https://pethelpful.com

http://www.seniorlink.co.nz

http://www.drsfostersmith.com

https://wagwalking.com

https://www.allaboutbirds.org

https://www.cuteness.com

www.training.ntwc.org

www.wildlifehealth.org

http://animaldiversity.org

http://healthypets.mercola.com

http://www.kijiji.ca

http://www.marshallpet.com

https://www.all-about-Monk Parakeets.com

Copyright and Trademarks: This publication is Copyrighted 2018 by Pesa Publishing. All products, publications, software and services mentioned and recommended in this publication are protected by trademarks. In such instance, all trademarks & copyright belong to the respective owners. All rights reserved. No part of this book may be reproduced or transferred in any form or by any means, graphic, electronic, or mechanical, including photocopying, recording, taping, or by any information storage retrieval system, without the written permission of the authors. Pictures used in this book are either royalty free pictures bought from stock-photo websites or have the source mentioned underneath the picture.

Disclaimer and Legal Notice: This product is not legal or medical advice and should not be interpreted in that manner. You need to do your own due-diligence to determine if the content of this product is right for you. The author and the affiliates of this product are not liable for any damages or losses associated with the content in this product. While every attempt has been made to verify the information shared in this publication, neither the author nor the affiliates assume any responsibility for errors, omissions or contrary interpretation of the subject matter herein. Any perceived slights to any specific person(s) or organization(s) are purely unintentional. We have no control over the nature, content and availability of the web sites listed in this book. The inclusion of any web site links does not necessarily imply a recommendation or endorse the views expressed within them. Pesa Publishing takes no responsibility for, and will not be liable for, the websites being temporarily unavailable or being removed from the Internet. The accuracy and completeness of information provided herein and opinions stated herein are not guaranteed or warranted to produce any particular results, and the advice and strategies, contained herein may not be suitable for every individual. The author shall not be liable for any loss incurred as a consequence of the use and application, directly or indirectly, of any information presented in this work. This publication is designed to provide information in regards to the subject matter covered. The information included in this book has been compiled to give an overview of the subject s and detail some of the symptoms, treatments etc. that are available to people with this condition. It is not intended to give medical advice. For a firm diagnosis of your condition, and for a treatment plan suitable for you, you should consult your doctor or consultant. The writer of this book and the publisher are not responsible for any damages or negative consequences following any of the treatments or methods highlighted in this book. Website links are for informational purposes and should not be seen as a personal endorsement; the same applies to the products detailed in this book. The reader should also be aware that although the web links included were correct at the time of writing, they may become out of date in the future.